# ONE-POT MEDITERRANEAN DIET

# One-Pot
# MEDITERRANEAN
# DIET

## 101 Simple Meals for Your Skillet, Baking Sheet, Dutch Oven, and More

**Kenton Kotsiris and
Jane Kotsiris**

**Photography by Darren Muir**

ROCKRIDGE
PRESS

For general information on our other products and services or to obtain technical support, please contact our Customer Care Department within the United States at (866) 744-2665, or outside the United States at (510) 253-0500.

Rockridge Press publishes its books in a variety of electronic and print formats. Some content that appears in print may not be available in electronic books, and vice versa.

Interior and Cover Designer: Jill Lee
Art Producer: Meg Baggott
Editor: Jed Bickman
Production Manager: Riley Hoffman
Production Editor: Sigi Nacson

Photography © 2020 Darren Muir
Author photo courtesy of © Camarie McBride

ISBN: Print 978-1-64739-242-0 | Ebook 978-1-64739-243-7

R0

To friends and family
and all those who've encouraged us
to be enthusiastic at-home chefs.
We could not have
created this without you.

# Contents

# Introduction

We are Kenton and Jane, a married couple living in Southern California who love to cook and explore Mediterranean cuisine. Mediterranean cooking has special meaning in our lives, even though we were first introduced to this cuisine in different ways.

Kenton has Greek, Italian, and Irish heritage and grew up in a Greek Orthodox household in Southern California. His family taught him how to maintain cultural traditions through religion and cooking delicious and authentic Greek meals. He was immersed in Mediterranean ingredients and flavor profiles that continue to influence much of his cooking as an adult.

Jane has an Eastern and Western European background and always loved cooking with her family as a young girl in Southern California. While in high school, Jane met her lifelong best friend, Helen, whose family introduced her to North African and Middle Eastern cuisine. She continues to try to incorporate those flavor profiles into her cooking.

When we met during our undergraduate studies at UCLA, we immediately knew our unique backgrounds and openness to different cultures would make for an extraordinary connection. Upon graduation, we moved to the United Kingdom to obtain our master's degrees, and our love of travel and food blossomed even further. During our time in Europe, we visited Italy, Egypt, and Greece. We enjoyed cured meats in Sicily, stuffed grape leaves in Egypt, and souvlaki in Greece. The explosion of fresh flavors offered in different parts of the Mediterranean was enticing, and we were completely hooked.

A few years after our travels, we longed to document our passion for food and culinary experiences and decided a blog would be an ideal way to do so. We wanted to share our family recipes and stay engaged with Mediterranean cuisine while juggling our busy schedules. Our website, www.lemonandolives.com, is mainly about Greek cuisine, but we never lost sight of the Mediterranean lifestyle we wanted to embrace. But we faced endless obstacles to staying on track with our Mediterranean diet. We loved cooking but hated the cleanup. We adored flavorful and robust dishes but didn't like searching for hard-to-find ingredients. We wanted to enjoy the foods we loved, but this way of eating had to fit into our everyday lives, and not just our blog posts.

When we realized many of our favorite meals used only one cooking vessel, we had the answer. One-pot cooking kept the spirit of the Mediterranean diet alive while cutting the time we spent in the kitchen. Prepping meals ahead, using limited ingredients, and cooking in one pot were key to staying healthy without sacrificing the delicious foods we love. Thus, this book was brought to life.

Our one-pot Mediterranean diet cookbook is a unique way to stay fit and healthy, cook simple and flavorful dishes, and avoid spending lots of time in the kitchen. We hope this book introduces you to well-known and more obscure Mediterranean dishes reimagined with fewer ingredients and one cooking vessel. We hope our unique backgrounds and love for cooking shine through these recipes, and that you will come to enjoy them all.

# CHAPTER ONE

# The Mediterranean Diet Made Easy

The Mediterranean diet, which we like to call a "lifestyle" in our home, includes foods from the many countries that surround the Mediterranean Sea. In the 1960s, scientists researched why Greeks and Italians lived longer and had fewer chronic health issues than many others around the world. They found that people in these countries (and in other Mediterranean regions) shared a similar lifestyle, which included exercise, mainly in the form of walking, a relaxed pace of life, and a diet of healthy whole foods. What's more, while many of the countries in this region prepared similar dishes, they all used seasonal, fresh local ingredients and spices. So, cultural dishes took on different nuances depending on the geography despite shared access to the Mediterranean Sea. Scientists realized that some main commonalities identified the Mediterranean diet and lifestyle as unique to these countries. In the next section, we will discuss the basics of the Mediterranean diet.

# Basics of the Mediterranean Diet

The Mediterranean diet is composed of foods from many different countries and thus offers a wide variety of ingredient choices. Beyond the diversity of foods, it's also essential to understand how people living in these regions organize their meals. A plant-based approach is an underlying theme for following this healthy lifestyle, and the Mediterranean diet food pyramid places red meat right at the top, alongside sweets, in the smallest category. (Yes, red meats and sweets are in the same category of food, and you should eat them only about once a week.)

So, if red meat is off-limits most nights, what's the plan for the rest of the week when you're following the Mediterranean diet? That's a great question! In this diet, vegetables are the star of the show. Your plate is going to be full of vegetables, alongside legumes, seafood, and some nuts. You can include other meats a few times a week as well.

Overall, the pyramid from the ground up is as follows (most frequent to least frequent):

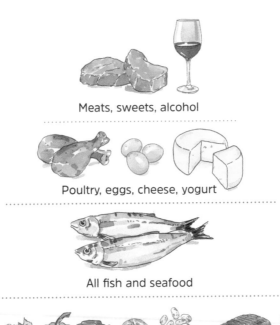

Meats, sweets, alcohol

Poultry, eggs, cheese, yogurt

All fish and seafood

Fruits, vegetables, grains, legumes. beans, nuts. olive oil, herbs, spices

Physical activity for 30 minutes a day

To follow the Mediterranean diet, tiers 1 and 2 are your daily choices, and tier 3 contains foods to include just a few days a week. The Mediterranean diet encourages eating a vegetarian meal at least one day a week. If you are unfamiliar with vegetarian cuisine, that may seem challenging at first, but as you explore this cookbook, this guideline will be easy to follow and may become something you enjoy.

The primary source of fat in this lifestyle is olive oil, which is used in everything from cooking to drizzling over salads and spreads. Olive oil is a good source of mono-unsaturated fats, which are healthier than the saturated fats found in butter, lard, meat, and dairy. You'll also encounter these healthy fats in the handful of nuts you can consume per day. One thing to keep in mind is that both olive oil and nuts are high-calorie foods, so do not overindulge in them.

Before we move on to the next section, here are a few things to keep in mind when shopping, planning, and cooking on your Mediterranean diet journey.

In most grocery stores, the center sections are processed-food territory. The heart of this diet is fresh, whole foods, so you'll find most of the items (not including legumes, nuts, and whole grains) around the perimeter of the grocery store and in the produce section. Also, whenever possible, choose seasonal fruits and vegetables because they taste better and are usually on sale or cheaper than out-of-season produce.

When it comes to planning, let what's in season or on sale guide you. Be respectful of your budget, because if this lifestyle gets expensive, you might not continue it, and that would negatively impact your overall health. Also, when planning your meals, consider recipes you can make ahead to store for those days when you're short on time. Look for tips in the recipes to help you with make-ahead meals.

Lastly, when it comes to cooking, don't be afraid to alter recipes to suit your needs. The most important thing you can do is cook whole foods, lots of vegetables, and nothing processed. If you've made healthy choices when shopping and planning, cooking should be easy. Always cook what you have on hand to minimize waste. Got a bunch of vegetables about to go bad? This is the perfect time to make a healthy veggie soup.

## FOODS TO FOCUS ON

As illustrated earlier, there are four tiers in the Mediterranean diet food pyramid.

The largest tier consists of beans, rice, grains, fruits, and vegetables. These ingredients are consumed most frequently during the week, and they are found in many dishes throughout this book. There are also plant-based substitutions for certain meat recipes, so you can adapt your meals if needed to follow the vegetarian or vegan base of the pyramid.

The second tier is fish and seafood. These very healthy proteins should be included in meals two or three times a week. It can be intimidating to cook whole pieces of fish, but don't worry—the recipes in this book make it simple to incorporate fish and seafood into delicious meals.

Poultry, eggs, cheese, and yogurt represent the third tier. Eat these foods in moderate portions a few times throughout the week. You will find most of the egg, cheese, and yogurt options in the Breakfasts and Desserts chapters of this book.

The last tier of the pyramid includes meat and sweets. Red meat encompasses steak, lamb, pork, bison, elk, and venison. When following the Mediterranean diet, you should consume these foods least often; try to limit how frequently you eat them, or, at a minimum, have smaller portions.

## FOODS TO CUT BACK ON

Quick and easy meals always bring to mind fast food, processed food, and prepackaged food, but in the Mediterranean diet, these choices are avoided whenever possible. These foods are often altered from their natural state to make them tastier, cheaper, and more easily consumed. Processed and prepackaged foods often have additives such as artificial coloring, artificial flavors, sodium, sugar (in many forms), and saturated fats (until 2018, they were also likely to contain health-damaging trans fats, but these have since been banned in the United States). This is obviously the antithesis of a healthy, balanced diet focused on whole, fresh foods. This book reimagines quick and easy meals with a one-pot method that uses fewer ingredients than traditional recipes and involves far less preparation and cleanup.

Health food stores, as well as grocery stores, often have healthier prepackaged or less-processed options that do not contain the additives mentioned earlier. These products can be used if whole, fresh ingredients are not available. This means purchasing flash-frozen spinach instead of fresh greens for a side dish, precooked chicken for a delicious soup, or even organic sodium-free canned legumes. We want to emphasize the importance of eating fresh, whole foods while you're following the Mediterranean diet, but saving time and sticking to a budget are also of enormous value.

# Health Benefits

You have probably heard about the benefits of the Mediterranean diet. It's consistently ranked as one of the best diets in the world, and many doctors recommend it. The Mediterranean diet has been shown to:

- Help manage depression

- Help manage rheumatoid arthritis

- Help manage type 2 diabetes

- Help prevent Alzheimer's disease and cognitive decline

- Increase longevity

- Reduce the risk of Parkinson's disease

- Reduce the risk of cancer

- Reduce the risk of heart disease

- Reduce the risk of stroke

- Support agility in older adults

- Support weight-loss goals and help maintain healthy body mass

But of course, a diet is only as healthy as the food you eat while you're on it, so to get these health benefits, you have to stick to this way of eating, and that's where the Mediterranean lifestyle really shines. This diet is so effective in large part because of the straightforward approach it takes to food.

For starters, the Mediterranean diet does not include any processed foods. When you eliminate processed products from your diet, you also remove the preservatives and other unwanted additives they contain, which our bodies shouldn't be exposed to. The Mediterranean diet is all about eating fresh, whole foods, including lots of fruits and vegetables. Additionally, you will be cooking nutritious meals at home, which supports good health and is budget-friendly, versus eating at fast-food restaurants or getting takeout.

The Mediterranean diet is easy to follow because it does not require counting calories or eating bland, restrictive meals. You will not be left hungry at the end of the day with few to no calories left in your daily allotment. And you will never be forced to watch other people eat something that tastes good while you pick at your special diet food. Meals prepared following the guidelines of this lifestyle are vibrant, flavorful, and nutritionally balanced.

The only thing you have to focus on is eating healthy whole foods and vegetables. That's it. You'll be able to enjoy real food, with lots of variety to boot, like a fresh salad with a tasty olive oil dressing and tempting linguine and clams one night, and chicken with legumes in a rich tomato sauce the next night. One thing you'll notice is that when you consume healthy foods, you feel full more quickly, so you may end up eating less but will never feel deprived.

Remember, the health benefits of any diet or eating plan are useful only if you're able to stick with it. Two of the main reasons people cannot stick with a plan are difficulty and time. The Mediterranean diet is not difficult in the slightest. It requires you to buy healthy ingredients and steer clear of processed foods. Also, this book will provide you with a fantastic base of healthy, Mediterranean diet–friendly dishes that take very little time to prepare using the one-pot method. With the recipes in this book, you're going to become a rock star in the kitchen, improve your health, and spend quality time with your family and friends, all while cooking delicious meals in record time. We've even included some recipes that take 30 minutes or less!

# One-Pot Cooking Makes the Mediterranean Diet Easy

The one-pot way of cooking is common in many of the countries that make up the Mediterranean region. The foods in the diet are simple, seasonal, fresh, and not processed. This enables people to cook foods quickly and blend ingredients together simply and effectively. Thus, this way of life and the routine needed to follow the diet successfully are a perfect match for one-pot cooking. When you cook in one pot, the flavors and seasonings come together in delicious and exceptional ways. For example, think of your favorite soups and stews: their delightful flavor profiles are the result of simmering the ingredients together in one pot.

Recently, there has been a resurgence of interest in one-pot cooking, and not just the expected recipes, such as soups and casseroles. Many recipes push the boundaries of this method by using a variety of cooking vessels and trying new combinations of techniques and ingredients. The driving force behind these changes is our busy lifestyle. On a Wednesday night, when you're tired or the kids are hungry or washing 15 dishes is not appealing, the concept of one-pot cooking is a lifesaver. The ease of using one pot means you could make a meal from start to finish in less than 30 minutes and, in some cases, be left with only one dish to be washed. Who doesn't love making a delicious, healthy dinner that's quick and easy, and requires minimal cleanup?

Beyond maximizing your time in the kitchen, there's also an important concept at play in the Mediterranean diet. Maybe you are already familiar with the health benefits of the Mediterranean diet, or your doctor recommended the plan and you're ready to try it. When you're beginning a journey to change the way you eat, the more complicated that journey seems, the harder it is to stick with it. When a diet or lifestyle change is simple, you're more likely to follow through with it, and then all those amazing health benefits we mentioned earlier can be obtained. That's what happens when you blend the Mediterranean diet with one-pot cooking.

The real question then becomes, what delicious foods are you going to cook? It's no longer a question of fitting the plan into your busy lifestyle, but of which region of the Mediterranean you will explore tonight. It is a culinary trip that is full of health and weight-loss benefits. Not only do you get to cook fresh, healthy foods, but you also get to do it all in one pot.

In the next section, we'll explore the diverse regions of the Mediterranean and discover their unique staple foods and flavor profiles.

# Regions, Tastes, and Cultures

One of the things that makes Mediterranean cuisine so amazing is the unique culinary diversity of the region. The Mediterranean Sea has been heavily sailed for as long as humans have built boats—sometimes for exploration and trade, other times for war. However, the one reason for travel that has remained constant is the transportation of culture and food.

When the dynamics of the Mediterranean diet are broken down, it is apparent that it extends beyond Italy and Greece, arguably the two countries most often cited as exemplary. But the Mediterranean also includes parts of North Africa, Spain, France, and the Middle East, and each of these regions sailed to the others, transferring their own cooking methods and dishes and returning home from their travels with new techniques. This dynamic process created one of the most diverse food cultures the world has ever known.

A perfect example of this process is couscous, a staple in North Africa, where many countries claim it as their national dish. Today, couscous is cooked throughout the Mediterranean. Moreover, you could travel to many regions highlighted in this book and find it prepared differently. This is why the Mediterranean diet is so unique, and why there are endless possibilities for creating simple, healthy dishes. All you have to do is look to a country that also shares the Mediterranean shoreline for inspiration.

Now that you understand Mediterranean cuisine encompasses many different nations, you might be thinking, "But what does this food taste like?" Well, it's delicious, obviously! Mediterranean cuisine features fresh, vibrant, seasonal fruits and vegetables accented with many herbs and spices. Alongside these, you're able to indulge in whole grains, pasta, and legumes. This bounty of exceptional ingredients comes together in the form of nutritious whole-food meals that are good for your body.

It is time to explore the countries that inspire our one-pot Mediterranean diet recipes. Keep in mind that the focus is on the areas of a country or region touching the shoreline of the Mediterranean Sea, and not necessarily the country as a whole. Cooking methods change, sometimes drastically, the farther you move away from the Mediterranean. There are many regions along the Mediterranean Sea that follow the Mediterranean diet, but this book focuses on or takes inspiration from the following areas.

■ Western Europe    ■ From the Ionian Sea to the Aegean Sea    ■ From the Bosporus to the Red Sea    ■ North Africa

## WESTERN EUROPE

This area includes parts of Spain and the South of France.

In eastern Spain, Valencian cuisine features heaps of rice and a plethora of seafood. A perfect example would be the ever-popular paella. In this dish, you can see the influence of the Mediterranean firsthand because as you move farther away from the ocean, the proteins change from seafood to meat. Herbs and spices commonly used in this part of Spain include saffron, bay leaf, rosemary, paprika, and garlic. Since many citrus trees grow in the region, these fruits find their way into many dishes as well.

The South of France features many fish-based dishes, but we tend to see them served with vegetables in place of rice, like cod with tomatoes and garlic. You'll also find rich dishes like chicken with mushroom sauce. In addition to heavy use of olive oil, you'll find many recipes that call for onions, shallots, parsley, tomatoes, fennel, thyme, rosemary, oregano, and garlic.

## FROM THE IONIAN SEA TO THE AEGEAN SEA

This area includes Italy and Greece.

Italy and Greece are blessed with an extensive coastline bordering the Mediterranean Sea, so a large percentage of their foods are influenced by this proximity. Some people argue that only Southern Italy should be included when considering the Mediterranean diet, but the characteristics of the diet do extend beyond the central areas.

Italy is the land of pizza and pasta, but it has so much more to offer. Don't worry—those popular dishes do conform to the Mediterranean diet, and you'll find several fabulous pizza and pasta recipes in this book. Margherita pizza and *spaghetti alle vongole* (spaghetti with clams) are just two pleasing choices. You will also discover delicious dishes like sautéed shrimp topped with tomatoes, white beans, and garlic, and *minestra maritata* (Italian wedding soup). Beyond relying on a lot of olive oil, seafood, and vegetables, Italian cuisine also uses basil, sage, rosemary, fennel, and oregano to elevate dishes.

Historically, Greece has given us democracy and philosophy, but it's also contributed many spectacular, healthy Mediterranean recipes. You can do no wrong by enjoying a traditional Greek salad, known as a *horiatiki* salad. This lovely dish contains no lettuce, just lots of healthy vegetables dressed with olive oil and topped with a sprinkling of oregano and creamy feta cheese. Leftover fish shines in regional fish stew, and you can round off a satisfying meal with *sfakianopita* (Cretan cheese pie) or simple pan-roasted almonds and honey for dessert. Fish and vegetables play a significant role in almost every dish, especially on the Greek islands. To add flavor to their meals, Greeks tend to use a lot of oregano, rosemary, olives, olive oil, feta, lemon, garlic, and thyme.

## FROM THE BOSPORUS TO THE RED SEA

This region includes Turkey, Syria, and Lebanon.

When studying the different countries in this region, you will find a lot of similar dishes. The main differences are the type of seasoning used and whether the dish is vegetable- or meat-based. One of the most popular Turkish recipes is *menemen*, a delicious egg-and-tomato-based dish mixed with spices and served with bread, similar to shakshuka. Another well-liked dish is *kuru fasulye*, a tomato-based stew with white beans. Some herbs and spices commonly used in Turkey are sumac, mint, oregano, and cumin.

The foods of Syria and Lebanon fall into a subcategory called Levantine cuisine. These countries are not often combined politically, but they do feature many of the same dishes. Southern Turkey has similar recipes, so this area can also be included in Levantine cuisine. These regions utilize a unique seasoning blend called za'atar, which is becoming more widely available in the United States (you can even make your own za'atar blend at home—see page 31). Za'atar can be used to season everything from meats and fish to yogurt and yogurt spreads like labneh as well as breads like *man'oushe*, a za'atar-topped flatbread. Levantine cuisine also features many healthy side dishes, such as tabbouleh, and many delicious lentil-based soups. Some common spices in Levantine cooking are cumin, turmeric, cinnamon, cardamom, nutmeg, sumac, aniseed, and the aforementioned za'atar.

## NORTH AFRICA

In North Africa, as in the Levant, the native dishes of different countries have been blended to create a distinct cooking style called Maghreb (Maghrebi) cuisine. This area includes the northernmost parts of Africa that have a Mediterranean shoreline, such as Libya, Tunisia, Algeria, and Morocco. This culinary region also includes Egypt because it shares many similar dishes and ingredients.

Couscous might be the first thing you think of when considering North African food. Not only do most people love it, but it can also be prepared in so many ways. Couscous is lovely as a plain side dish but can also be mixed with vegetables and legumes. It makes a scrumptious dessert as well. Couscous is an incredibly versatile food perfectly suited to the Mediterranean diet. This region also gives us dishes like lamb and bean stew, and if you're in the mood for something spicy, look to harissa, a spice paste that is added to just about everything in Tunisia. Harissa perks up any dish, from meats and stews to couscous. Maghreb cuisine also features spices such as ginger, paprika, cinnamon, saffron, cumin, and aniseed.

Moreover, you'll find countless vegetarian recipes using various legumes, which are a staple of the Mediterranean diet. Egyptian dishes are often flavored with cumin, mint, coriander, and aniseed.

Overall, many different nations make up Mediterranean cuisine. The cuisine highlights the overlapping similarities of the regional recipes, and the differences in spices or base ingredients from place to place give us the ability to be adventurous. Merely altering one spice, vegetable, or protein means we enjoy another country's spin on a healthy Mediterranean meal.

# The Mediterranean Kitchen

As mentioned earlier, the ingredients you will need for the recipes in this book will be whole, fresh foods, and we will avoid the use of processed items. We also want you to make use of a variety of spices and herbs, as these are the wonderful additions that bring a recipe to life! These herbs and spices include (but are not limited to) salt, pepper, garlic powder, onion powder, sumac, za'atar, red pepper flakes, chili powder, Italian seasoning, rosemary, thyme, and oregano, to name a few. While most people have salt and pepper on hand, we recommend that you purchase the other herbs and spices listed before cooking some of the recipes in the book.

# IN THE PANTRY

Here are a few ingredients called for frequently throughout this book.

**Extra-virgin olive oil (EVOO):** Extra-virgin olive oil (as opposed to regular olive oil) is used when the taste of the oil is important. This oil is from pure cold-pressed olives and has a green color and grassy, fruity, slightly peppery taste. It is used for drizzling and often for vinaigrettes or recipes where it is not heated.

**Regular olive oil:** This olive oil is less expensive than EVOO and is a blend of cold-pressed olive oil and refined olive oil, which is treated to remove impurities. It has a neutral taste and is a pale gold color. Regular olive oil is best used for pan-frying and sautéing.

**Legumes:** Legumes include different colored lentils, peas, navy beans, chickpeas, black beans, and split peas, to name a few. Beans and lentils are used extensively in salads, stews, soups, and many other Mediterranean diet recipes. Low-sodium, organic canned and dried legumes should both be available in your pantry.

**Whole grains:** There are many different types of whole grains to choose from, and while each has a distinct flavor and texture, they can usually be substituted for one another in recipes. Whole grains include rice, quinoa, farro, bulgur, and wheat berries as well as items made with whole grains such as breads, tortillas, couscous, and pasta.

**Olives:** What would Mediterranean cuisine be without olives?! This fruit belongs to the same family as mangos, almonds, cherries, and pistachios. They are picked both ripe and unripe, which can determine the color of the fruit: unripe olives are green, and ripe olives can be either black or green. Olives are cured and fermented after being picked both ripe and unripe. The flavor of the varieties is unique, so try them all.

**Dried herbs and spices:** Herbs and spices are the cornerstone of Mediterranean cooking, and you will be using many different ones to create delectable meals. Some popular herbs include oregano, rosemary, basil, thyme, marjoram, and chives; popular spices include red pepper flakes, allspice, cinnamon, cumin, cardamom, coriander, and nutmeg.

**Canned tomatoes:** There are some wonderful-quality canned tomatoes you can use when fresh aren't an option. Whenever possible, look for D.O.P. San Marzano tomatoes, a variety certified as having grown in a specific Italian region. These tomatoes are bright red, sweet, and flavorful.

# IN THE REFRIGERATOR AND FREEZER

**Fresh produce:** As you learned earlier, vegetables and fruits are the foundation of the Mediterranean diet, so you will want to stock your refrigerator with a bounty of choices. This book uses many different types, but the most common are onions, garlic, tomatoes, cucumber, bell peppers, carrots, leeks, mushrooms, zucchini, berries, peaches, and melon.

**Fresh herbs:** Fresh herbs are used as a lovely garnish or in salads or uncooked dishes. We like parsley, rosemary, basil, and thyme.

**Fish and seafood:** It makes sense that a diet that is all about the Mediterranean region would highlight fresh fish and seafood. You don't have to stock these ingredients in your refrigerator all the time—it is better to buy fish and seafood fresh no earlier than the day before you plan to cook it. Look for cod, halibut, mahi-mahi, trout, haddock, clams, mussels, and shrimp.

**Yogurt:** This ingredient is eaten often in this diet, so, for example, make sure you have a couple of containers of full-fat Greek yogurt on hand for dips, breakfasts, toppings, and desserts.

**Cheeses:** Manchego, feta, Parmesan, mozzarella, and goat cheese are used in many recipes in this book. The portion sizes are not excessive, so using these cheeses still meets the Mediterranean diet guidelines.

---

## ON THE COUNTER

Not everything you use when cooking needs to be locked away in your pantry or refrigerator. Let's talk about the wonderful things that are best kept out on the counter. What would Mediterranean food be without the addition of lemon, limes, oranges, and grapefruit? You can spruce up so many recipes by simply adding a bit of citrus zest or a squirt of juice. These fruits can be left out in a pretty bowl (citrus is easier to juice when it's at room temperature, too). Tomatoes can also be stored on the counter because they are best when picked a little green and then ripened off the vine. Avocados ripen after harvest, especially when placed in a paper bag with a banana or two. They should be used within a day or two of ripening.

# The One-Pot Kitchen

Making quick, foolproof meals that leave you plenty of time to sit down, relax, and enjoy your day probably doesn't sound like any type of diet. In fact, diets are often more work than less, and can be a struggle to maintain. We are here to change that. By prepping items ahead of time and using limited ingredients and a one-pot cooking method, this cookbook illustrates that the Mediterranean diet lifestyle is easy, attainable, and satisfying. These are all crucial elements for following—and sticking to—a new set of habits in the kitchen.

By only using one pot, you guarantee that cleanup is quick, eliminating the need for the arduous scrubbing of multiple pots and pans after a single meal. People are often too busy to get through most of their daily tasks, let alone spend hours in the kitchen sweating over meals or washing dishes afterward. One-pot cooking is going to free up your time and make preparing a delicious meal a pleasure rather than a chore.

In this book, you will also learn that different meals or dishes work better in different vessels. It may be one-pot cooking, but it's not one-pot-fits-all cooking. We've included different techniques for each vessel to shorten the time you spend prepping and cooking. For example, if you usually cook vegetables in one baking dish and chicken in another, you can instead layer both on a baking sheet and cut the cooking time in half.

You might be thinking, "Wait, I can use just a baking sheet to make a whole meal?" Yes! In fact, let's take a look at what "one pot" means in the scope of this book. One-pot cooking is cooking in *one main vessel*, which could be anything from a saucepan to a baking sheet to a Dutch oven, a variety of cookware you probably already own. Here are eight of the most common vessels found in an average home kitchen.

**Skillet:** This versatile pan, also known as a frying pan, is often 8 to 12 inches in diameter with a long handle and low, sloped sides. It does not usually come with a lid; however, lids can be purchased separately. Many different types of skillets are available, including cast-iron skillets, French skillets, two-handled skillets, and nonstick skillets, to name just a few. For most of the recipes in this book, you will need a 10-inch nonstick skillet. Use this pan to stir-fry, pan-fry, or sauté. Skillets are perfect when you need to move ingredients around easily and don't need a lid.

**Sauté pan:** This vessel is designed for lower heat and has higher, straight sides compared with a skillet. Sauté pans have a long handle and usually come with a lid. A sauté pan is excellent for liquid cooking methods, which is why the size is measured in quarts versus inches. On average, a sauté pan holds between 2 and 4 quarts of liquid. You can use this pan for poaching, braising, and wilting greens. The shape paired with the lid allows for slower evaporation of liquid.

**Saucepan:** Saucepans are deep vessels with high, straight sides. Depending on their size, they can hold between 1 and 6 quarts of liquid. Saucepans have a long handle, just like skillets and sauté pans. The smaller cooking surface of the saucepan produces even heat, and the higher sides mean liquid stays contained. Use a saucepan to make soup for two, cook quinoa, poach eggs, or blanch vegetables.

**Stockpot:** This is probably the largest pot in your kitchen and is ideal for soups and stews. Stockpots hold a much higher volume of liquid than their smaller cousin, the saucepan. Because of its versatility, a stockpot can be used for anything from making a double batch of your favorite Italian ragù to simmering an entire chicken with vegetables, with room to spare. An average-size stockpot can hold 8 to 10 quarts (though some can be much larger, holding 20 quarts or more), and is traditionally tall and narrow.

**Dutch oven:** Often constructed of enameled cast iron, this heavy-duty lidded pot can go straight from the stovetop to the oven, increasing its versatility. Dutch ovens deliver consistent, even heat and, when covered with their lid, retain the moisture of the food. Use a Dutch oven for braising, making stews, or even deep-frying.

**Baking sheet:** Baking sheets come in many sizes and several shapes. Most home ovens can fit only a half sheet pan (13 by 18 inches), but larger full sheet pans (18 by 26 inches) as well as smaller quarter sheet pans (9 by 13 inches) are also available. Baking sheets, also referred to as sheet pans or baking trays, usually have a low 1-inch rim around the sides, which helps circulate air around the food. A baking sheet without a rim or with one or two sides turned up at a slight angle is known as a cookie sheet; be sure to use a rimmed baking sheet, not a cookie sheet, for the recipes in this book. There are endless possibilities of what can be cooked on a baking sheet.

**Baking dish:** Baking dishes come in many different sizes, but the size most commonly used for one-pot cooking is 9 by 13 inches, which holds about 4 quarts. Baking dishes are used for making casseroles or lasagna and for roasting meats and vegetables. For recipes that go right from the oven to the table, then into the refrigerator after the meal, baking dishes are an ideal cooking vessel. They can be made from metal, glass, ceramic, or silicone.

**Roasting pan:** Roasting pans are usually made of metal and often come with a metal rack that fits into the pan, which allows juices from meat cooking on the rack to drip to the bottom of the pan for easy basting. They come in several sizes, usually ranging from 10 to 18 inches, and can be rectangular or oval. Compared to baking dishes and baking sheets, roasting pans have higher sides, which allows for higher retention of heat around the food. You can use a roasting pan to cook a chicken, roast large vegetables such as spaghetti squash or butternut squash, or even make fun meals like deep-dish pizza.

This is a one-pot cookbook, but you'll need a few other pieces of kitchen equipment to prep the items you'll be cooking in that one vessel.

Some basic kitchen tools include:

- Box grater
- Can opener
- Colander
- Cutting board (or two)
- Immersion blender or regular standing blender
- Knives
- Measuring cups (liquid and dry) and measuring spoons
- Spatula (silicone or otherwise heatproof)
- Stainless steel mixing bowls
- Tongs
- Vegetable peeler

It is nice to have the following equipment:

- Grill
- Food processor
- Meat thermometer
- Mixer, handheld or stand
- Spiralizer

# About the Recipes

You're about to embark on a one-pot Mediterranean diet journey, and we are so thrilled that you've decided to embrace this lifestyle of healthy eating. Before you venture on to the recipes, here is an overview of how to properly use the book.

First and foremost, your kitchen is your kitchen. You make the rules, and more important, you know what you and your family's preferences are. If a recipe calls for a spice or ingredient you do not like, then skip it. Remember, besides making recipes simple with the one-pot method, they must also taste good, or you will not continue on your Mediterranean diet journey.

This also goes hand in hand with trips to the store. A healthy Mediterranean diet should not mean more time shopping. If you don't have a specific ingredient, do you have something similar you could use instead? Maybe this is the perfect time to turn a meat-based dish into a vegetarian meal or to put a twist on your favorite recipe.

Another thing to consider is your budget. Whatever it is, stick to it. No matter the budget, you can make this diet work. So, buy seasonally whenever possible. Not sure what's in season? Look no further than your local produce person to point you in the right direction, or look for what's on sale or inexpensive because those items tend to be seasonal. As for fish, there are many different economical options, such as cod, tilapia, and haddock. For chicken and red meat, look at buying in bulk and freezing what you don't use right away.

Always think of your health and what's best for you. Just because something is good doesn't mean it's suitable for everyone. For example, a glass of wine with dinner is part of the Mediterranean way, but if you don't like wine, or have a health condition limiting this beverage, don't drink it. Also, before making a significant lifestyle change, discuss it with your doctor. Remember, do what's best for you and listen to your body.

## THE ONE-POT WAY

Throughout this book, you're going to find little icons that highlight the type of cooking vessel used in a recipe. If you're unsure what the icon represents, consult pages 14 to 16. Since we're highlighting this for you, it gives you the ability to search the recipes by cooking vessels. If you want to use your roasting pan, look for that icon and find the recipes that correspond to your needs. From there, you can make the decision on what recipe you want to try. Doing this may unlock some creative ideas, and it will also show you the versatility of your vessels.

## LABELS

In another attempt to make this cookbook as accessible as possible, and your life easy when it comes to cooking a healthy meal, we've added labels to the recipes. So if you're looking for a 30-minute meal or something with five ingredients or less, we've got them highlighted to help you.

## SUBSTITUTIONS AND TIPS

You're also going to discover little tips and tricks to help you as you go through the book. Where we can, we've offered up some tips on things like how to make a specific recipe vegetarian or how to take a vegetable-based dish and add some protein. We understand that sometimes people like variations, so we were mindful of that when creating these recipes. The recipe tips are to ensure your dish comes out amazing. For example, did you know that putting raw red onions in an ice bath before serving them reduces their bite? Interesting, right? Also, if something can be made ahead of time, we'll let you know. This allows you to prepare more complex recipes in less time after work.

We really hope you enjoy this book. We encourage you to give all the recipes a try, even if some are outside your comfort zone. The flavors you'll find might provide some great ideas on how to spice up your current favorites. You're about to discover how delicious unprocessed healthy whole foods and vegetables can be. We'll be there with you, giving you advice on the Mediterranean diet. We hope you're ready to experience the positive health benefits everyone keeps talking about!

Mediterranean Breakfast Board, *page 27*

# Breakfasts

# Pancetta Potato Hash

Serves: **4** | Prep time: **15 minutes** | Cook time: **19 minutes**

This hearty breakfast hash makes use of the microwave to cut cooking time, making it a delicious anytime option. The fresh vegetables, garlic, and olive oil are staples of the Mediterranean diet, and pancetta (salt-cured pork belly) is an Italian product made with different seasonings depending on the region. The pancetta adds flavor to this tasty hash without making this a meat-centric breakfast.

10½ ounces small potatoes (about 11)
2 tablespoons olive oil
2 garlic cloves, minced
Sea salt
Freshly ground black pepper

2 ounces cubed pancetta
1 pound asparagus, cut into 1-inch pieces
2 red bell peppers, coarsely chopped
⅛ teaspoon red pepper flakes

⅛ teaspoon Italian seasoning
4 large eggs
2 tablespoons water

1. Place the potatoes in a microwave-safe container with 2 tablespoons water, cover with a plate, and microwave on medium-high for 5 minutes, or until slightly fork-tender; drain if necessary.

2. In a large skillet, heat the olive oil over medium-high heat. Add the potatoes and garlic and season with salt and black pepper. Cook, stirring occasionally, for 4 minutes. Add the pancetta and cook for 2 minutes more. Add the asparagus, bell peppers, red pepper flakes, and Italian seasoning, and cook, stirring occasionally, for 4 to 5 minutes.

3. Reduce the heat to medium and create four wells in the mixture with the back of a spoon. Crack an egg into each well. Add the water, cover, and cook for 3 to 5 minutes, until the eggs are done to your preference. Remove from the heat and serve.

**SUBSTITUTION TIP:** Pancetta is the preferred choice for this dish because it's inexpensive and delicious. You can also make this dish vegetarian and add more of your favorite vegetables; just adjust the cooking time accordingly.

Per serving: Calories: 298; Total fat: 17g; Total carbs: 22g; Sugar: 5g; Protein: 16g; Fiber: 5g; Sodium: 358mg

# Egg and Pepper Pita

Serves: **4** | Prep time: **10 minutes** | Cook time: **10 minutes** | **30-Minute**

These warm, feel-good pitas have the perfect blend of fluffy eggs and colorful vegetables. When sautéing the vegetables, make sure all the excess liquid from the zucchini has evaporated, or your pitas will be soggy. If you enjoy a little heat, add more hot sauce to suit your taste. Hot sauce is one of the most versatile condiments in the world, and there are many different types available, from Tabasco to harissa to sambal oelek, so experiment until you land on a favorite.

2 pita breads

2 tablespoons olive oil

1 red or yellow bell pepper, diced

2 zucchini, quartered lengthwise and sliced

4 large eggs, beaten

Sea salt

Freshly ground black pepper

Pinch dried oregano

2 avocados, sliced

½ to ¾ cup crumbled feta cheese

2 tablespoons chopped scallion, green part only, for garnish

Hot sauce, for serving

1. In a large skillet, heat the pitas over medium heat until warmed through and lightly toasted, about 2 minutes. Remove the pitas from the skillet and set aside.

2. In the same skillet, heat the olive oil over medium heat. Add the bell pepper and zucchini and sauté for 4 to 5 minutes. Add the eggs and season with salt, black pepper, and the oregano. Cook, stirring, for 2 to 3 minutes, until the eggs are cooked through. Remove from the heat.

3. Slice the pitas in half crosswise and fill each half with the egg mixture. Divide the avocado and feta among the pita halves. Garnish with the scallion and serve with hot sauce.

**VARIATION TIP:** The egg mixture can also be wrapped in flour or corn tortillas instead of the pitas.

Per serving: Calories: 476; Total fat: 31g; Total carbs: 36g; Sugar: 8g; Protein: 17g; Fiber: 11g; Sodium: 455mg

# Shakshuka

Serves: **4** | Prep time: **10 minutes** | Cook time: **34 minutes**

Shakshuka, a delicious meal of eggs poached in a spiced tomato-and-vegetable sauce, is one of the signature breakfast dishes of North Africa and the Middle East, and it embodies the one-pot method.

2 tablespoons olive oil

1 small onion, diced

1 red or yellow bell pepper, coarsely chopped

4 garlic cloves, minced

2 teaspoons tomato paste

1 teaspoon harissa, or ¼ teaspoon red pepper flakes

¼ teaspoon ground cumin

¼ teaspoon paprika

¼ teaspoon sea salt

¼ teaspoon freshly ground black pepper

1 (12-ounce) jar roasted red peppers, plus 2 tablespoons brine from the jar

1 (15-ounce) can diced tomatoes with their juices

1 (15-ounce) can crushed tomatoes

1 bay leaf

4 large eggs

2 ounces goat cheese, for serving (optional)

6 or 7 basil leaves, for garnish (optional)

Pita bread, for serving (optional)

1. In a large sauté pan, heat the olive oil over medium-high heat. Add the onion and bell pepper and sauté until soft, 6 to 8 minutes. Add the garlic, tomato paste, harissa, cumin, paprika, salt, and black pepper. Cook for 2 to 3 minutes.

2. Add the roasted peppers and their brine, the diced tomatoes, crushed tomatoes, and bay leaf. Bring to a boil, reduce the heat to low, and simmer for 10 to 15 minutes, until the mixture thickens. Remove the bay leaf.

3. Make four shallow wells in the mixture with the back of a spoon and crack one egg into each well. Season each egg with salt and black pepper. Cover and simmer for 6 to 8 minutes, until the eggs are set.

4. Sprinkle with the goat cheese and garnish with the basil, if desired. Serve with pita alongside, if desired.

**STORAGE:** Store leftovers in an airtight container in the refrigerator for up to 2 days.

Per serving: Calories: 201; Total fat: 12g; Total carbs: 16g; Sugar: 8g; Protein: 9g; Fiber: 5g; Sodium: 468mg

# Blueberry-Banana Bowl with Quinoa

Serves: **4** | Prep time: **5 minutes** | Cook time: **20 minutes** | **30-Minute**

You might be surprised to learn that quinoa is an ideal breakfast grain, with balanced nutrition and a perfect flavor profile for a fruit bowl. Banana and blueberries add a pleasing sweetness and a splash of color to the dish. Blueberries are often called a superfood because they are bursting with antioxidants, high in fiber, and low on the glycemic index, which means they can help lower cholesterol when part of your regular diet. Look for wild blueberries for a change; they are smaller and have a more intense tangy-sweet flavor.

1½ cups water
¾ cup uncooked quinoa, rinsed
2 tablespoons honey, divided

1 cup blueberries (preferably frozen)
2 bananas (preferably frozen), sliced
½ cup sliced almonds or crushed walnuts

½ cup dried cranberries
1 cup granola
1 cup milk or nondairy milk of your choice

1. Combine the water and quinoa in a medium saucepan. Bring to a boil over medium-high heat, cover, reduce the heat to low, and simmer for 15 to 20 minutes, until the water has been absorbed. Remove from the heat and fluff the quinoa with a fork.

2. Evenly divide the quinoa among four bowls, about ½ cup for each bowl. Evenly divide the honey among the bowls and mix it in well. Top evenly with the blueberries, bananas, almonds, cranberries, granola, and milk. Serve.

**VARIATION TIP:** Try rolled oats, farro, wheat berries, millet, or any other whole grain in place of the quinoa for a delicious variation.

Per serving: Calories: 469; Total fat: 15g; Total carbs: 77g; Sugar: 33g; Protein: 12g; Fiber: 9g; Sodium: 31mg

# Greek Yogurt and Berries

Serves: **4** | Prep time: **5 minutes** | **No-Cook** | **30-Minute**

The simple title of this recipe is deceiving: this dish is a mélange of textures and flavors. Every spoonful has a different combination of crunchy granola, velvety yogurt, tart berries, sweet bananas, and honey. The simple preparation means you can be enjoying the dish in a few minutes, but you can also layer the ingredients in pretty glasses to create charming breakfast parfaits.

4 cups plain full-fat Greek yogurt

1 cup granola

½ cup blackberries

2 bananas, sliced and frozen

1 teaspoon chia seeds, for topping

1 teaspoon chopped fresh mint leaves, for topping

4 teaspoons honey, for topping (optional)

Evenly divide the yogurt among four bowls. Top with the granola, blackberries, bananas, chia seeds, mint, and honey (if desired), dividing evenly among the bowls. Serve.

**VARIATION TIP:** The toppings called for here can be swapped out for whatever you prefer, such as nuts, different fruit, or another sweetener. You can also use ricotta cheese in place of the yogurt.

Per serving: Calories: 283; Total fat: 9g; Total carbs: 42g; Sugar: 20g; Protein: 12g; Fiber: 5g; Sodium: 115mg

# Mediterranean Breakfast Board

Serves: **4 to 6** | Prep time: **15 minutes** | **No-Cook** | **30-Minute**

Mediterranean dining is all about the appreciation of good company and food lovingly prepared with whole, fresh ingredients. It is not unusual to sit down with family and friends for a meal and end up talking and laughing the hours away. This breakfast board, an exceptional spread of classic dishes, fruit, cheeses, meats, and condiments, inspires that type of gathering, and cutting out any cooking time allows you to linger.

½ cup Hummus (page 34)

½ cup Tabbouleh (page 40)

1 to 2 cups fresh fruit (such as grapes, sliced apples, blackberries, blueberries, etc.)

½ to ¾ cup assorted olives

¼ cup jam

6 Medjool dates, pitted

½ to 1 French baguette, cut into 10 to 12 slices

2 pita breads, cut into triangles

7 to 10 slices cheese, such as Manchego

1 (2-ounce) log goat cheese

10 to 12 slices cured meat (such as prosciutto, salami, etc.)

Place the hummus, tabbouleh, fruit, olives, and jam in individual small bowls and set them on a large serving platter. Arrange the dates, baguette, pita, sliced cheese, goat cheese, and cured meat on the platter around the bowls, creating an attractive spread. Serve.

VARIATION TIP: The ingredients can also be divided evenly among individual plates and served as an appetizer.

Per serving: Calories: 791; Total fat: 35g; Total carbs: 91g; Sugar: 38g; Protein: 30g; Fiber: 8g; Sodium: 1,532mg

# Crostini with Smoked Trout

Serves: **4** | Prep time: **10 minutes** | Cook time: **5 minutes** | **5-Ingredient** | **30-Minute**

Smoked fish is a common breakfast item in many countries, especially those near the ocean or, in this case, the Mediterranean Sea. Smoked salmon or herring is often the protein of choice, but trout is a delicious and underrated fish, complemented perfectly by luscious crème fraîche. The fresh dill elevates the flavor of this dish, even in such a small quantity. Don't be afraid to buy the large bunches of dill sold in most stores—the excess won't go to waste. Just separate the sprigs, freeze them on a baking sheet, transfer them to resealable plastic bags, and store in the freezer for up to 2 months.

½ French baguette, cut into 1-inch-thick slices

1 tablespoon olive oil

¼ teaspoon onion powder

1 (4-ounce) can smoked trout

¼ cup crème fraîche

¼ teaspoon chopped fresh dill, for garnish

1. Drizzle the bread on both sides with the olive oil and sprinkle with the onion powder.

2. Place the bread in a single layer in a large skillet and toast over medium heat until lightly browned on both sides, 3 to 4 minutes total.

3. Transfer the toasted bread to a serving platter and place 1 or 2 pieces of the trout on each slice. Top with the crème fraîche, garnish with the dill, and serve immediately.

**PREP TIP:** Instead of toasting the bread in a skillet, you can arrange the slices on a baking sheet and toast them under the broiler in a preheated oven until lightly browned on both sides, about 30 seconds per side.

Per serving: Calories: 206; Total fat: 10g; Total carbs: 15g; Sugar: 2g; Protein: 13g; Fiber: 1g; Sodium: 350mg

# Baked Cheese Pancake

Serves: **3 to 5** | Prep time: **30 minutes** | Cook time: **30 minutes**

When reading through this recipe, you might be reminded of blintzes, a traditional Jewish cheese-filled pancake that is incredibly difficult to get right without practice. This Mediterranean version is much simpler to prepare and has a fresh, sweet-and-salty bite that will have you coming back for more. Whip up these pancakes for a leisurely brunch and serve them with a platter of seasonal fruit and perhaps tall glasses of sparkling white wine.

1 cup water

2 large eggs

1 teaspoon honey

1 teaspoon olive oil

¾ cup all-purpose flour

2 tablespoons unsalted butter, melted

Freshly ground black pepper

6 ounces feta, crumbled, divided

1 tablespoon honey, for drizzling

1. Preheat the oven to 400°F. Line a baking sheet with parchment paper.

2. In a medium bowl, whisk together the water, eggs, honey, and olive oil until well combined.

3. Add the flour and melted butter and stir until well blended. Season with pepper. Cover the batter and let stand for 20 minutes, or until it thickens a bit.

4. Stir 4 ounces of feta into the batter, then pour the batter into the center of the prepared baking sheet (it will spread out into a circle) and sprinkle evenly with the remaining 2 ounces of feta.

5. Bake for 25 to 30 minutes, until golden brown.

6. Remove the baking sheet from the oven and cut the pancake into 3-inch squares or to the size and shape you prefer.

7. Serve drizzled with the honey.

COOKING TIP: While the batter sits, the flour will absorb more of the liquid, thickening the batter. Skipping this step and adding more flour to speed up the process may result in the flour altering the taste of the pancakes.

Per serving: Calories: 421; Total fat: 25g; Total carbs: 34g; Sugar: 10g; Protein: 16g; Fiber: 1g; Sodium: 629mg

# Avocado Toast Bites

Serves: **5** | Prep time: **10 minutes** | Cook time: **8 minutes** | **5-Ingredient** | **30-Minute**

If you enjoy looking up recipes, there is an excellent chance avocado toast has made an appearance in your searches. This unassuming dish has become a phenomenon because it's delicious, simple, and healthy. Many versions of avocado toast are similar to guacamole spread on bread, but this recipe has a pleasing complexity. Hints of heat and tartness accentuate the creamy avocado, and a drizzle of golden honey adds just the right sweetness.

½ French baguette
  (5 ounces), cut into
  ¼- to ½-inch-thick
  slices (about 25 slices)

3 medium avocados
Juice of ½ lemon
¼ teaspoon sea salt

1 tablespoon honey,
  for drizzling
¼ teaspoon red pepper
  flakes, for garnish

1.  Place the bread slices in a single layer in a large skillet and toast over medium-high heat for about 5 minutes, then flip and toast for about 3 minutes on the second side. Transfer the bread to a large plate.

2.  Scoop the avocado into a medium bowl and mash it with a potato masher or fork. Add the lemon juice and salt and mash to blend.

3.  Top each slice of bread with 1 teaspoon of the avocado mixture and drizzle evenly with the honey. Garnish with the red pepper flakes and serve.

**STORAGE:** Store any leftover avocado mixture in an airtight container in the refrigerator for up to 2 days. Assemble the toasts just before serving.

**PREP TIP:** Cut off about 1 inch from the top of the avocados if you are not sure they are ripe. You're looking for a nice bright green color and a soft texture.

Per serving: Calories: 310; Total fat: 19g; Total carbs: 33g; Sugar: 9g; Protein: 7g; Fiber: 11g; Sodium: 237mg

# Man'oushe, Two Ways | Cheese and Za'atar

**Serves: 4** | Prep time: **10 minutes** | Cook time: **5 minutes** | **5-Ingredient** | **30-Minute**

This is a traditional Levantine comfort food that makes a delicious and nourishing breakfast. *Za'atar* means "thyme" in Arabic, and it is a wonderful and flexible spice blend. Although the blend does contain thyme, it is the sumac in the mix that truly shines.

6 tablespoons za'atar, homemade (see Tip) or store-bought

¼ cup olive oil
4 pita breads

12 thin slices Manchego cheese

1. Preheat the oven to 400°F.

2. In a small bowl, stir together the za'atar and olive oil to form a paste.

3. Place the pitas on a baking sheet. Spread a thin layer of the za'atar mixture over 2 of the pitas and arrange the cheese slices on the remaining 2 pitas.

4. Bake for 3 to 5 minutes, until the cheese has melted.

5. Remove from the oven and let cool for a few minutes, then serve.

INGREDIENT TIPS: You can purchase za'atar in some stores or online, but you can also make your own with ⅓ cup dried thyme, 1 tablespoon ground sumac, 1 tablespoon sesame seeds, and 2 teaspoons dried marjoram. Adjust the ingredients to suit your palate; if sumac is not available, use lemon pepper seasoning or lemon zest.

Feel free to substitute your favorite cheese for the Manchego, or double either the cheese or the za'atar mixture to serve all pitas the same way. You could also cut the pitas into wedges to enjoy like a pizza!

Per serving: Calories: 353; Total fat: 26g; Total carbs: 18g; Sugar: 2g; Protein: 13g; Fiber: 2g; Sodium: 449mg

Skillet Asparagus with Lemon Zest and Red Pepper Flakes, *page 47*

# Salads, Soups, and Sides

# Hummus

A couple of decades ago, outside the Mediterranean region, hummus was only found on obscure ethnic menus, but this simple dip has become mainstream. It has always been a staple of Mediterranean cuisine. Its versatility and nutritional impact are undeniable. Hummus is an excellent protein, good any time of day, and ideal for dipping or spreading on any type of food. Once you start to make your own, you'll never want to buy it premade again.

1 (15-ounce) can
 chickpeas, drained
 and rinsed
½ cup tahini
Juice of 2 lemons
2 garlic cloves
2 tablespoons water
½ teaspoon sea salt,
 plus more as needed

¼ teaspoon paprika
¼ teaspoon ground
 cumin
¼ teaspoon freshly
 ground black pepper,
 plus more as needed
2 tablespoons olive
 oil, plus extra
 for drizzling

1 tablespoon pine nuts,
 for garnish
¼ teaspoon za'atar,
 homemade (see
 page 31) or
 store-bought,
 for garnish

1. In a food processor, combine the chickpeas, tahini, lemon juice, garlic, water, salt, paprika, cumin, and pepper and pulse for 30 seconds.

2. Add the olive oil and process for about 1 minute, until smooth.

3. Taste and adjust the seasoning. Serve the hummus drizzled with olive oil and garnished with the pine nuts and za'atar.

STORAGE: Store the dip in an airtight container in the refrigerator for up to 4 days.

VARIATION TIP: For a less tart flavor, reduce the lemon juice. Try using a different legume in place of the chickpeas, or add an assortment of herbs and spices or even a handful of dark leafy greens to change up the basic recipe.

Per serving: Calories: 464; Total fat: 33g; Total carbs: 34g; Sugar: 5g; Protein: 14g; Fiber: 10g; Sodium: 247mg

# Greek Cucumber-Yogurt Dip | Tzatziki

Serves: **6** | Prep time: **15 minutes** | **No-Cook** | **30-Minute**

Tzatziki is a ubiquitous side, sauce, dip, and condiment in Greece, and for a good reason. The refreshing flavor profile is the ideal companion to almost any hot meal. Garlic, a staple in nearly every cuisine in the world, adds a satisfying pungency. When purchasing garlic, choose heads that feel heavy for their size to ensure the cloves aren't dried out.

½ English cucumber, peeled and grated

2 cups plain full-fat Greek yogurt

3 tablespoons extra-virgin olive oil

Juice of 1 lemon

1 garlic clove, minced

2 tablespoons chopped fresh dill

1 to 2 teaspoons sea salt

1 teaspoon freshly ground black pepper

1 to 2 teaspoons red wine vinegar

1. Place the grated cucumber in a clean kitchen towel and twist the towel to squeeze out excess liquid, then place the cucumber in a large bowl.

2. Add the yogurt, olive oil, lemon juice, garlic, dill, salt, pepper, and vinegar and stir until well combined.

3. Taste and adjust the seasoning, then serve, or, if desired, refrigerate for a bit before serving to allow the flavors to mellow.

**STORAGE:** Store the tzatziki in an airtight container in the refrigerator for up to 4 days.

**PREP TIP:** Be sure to squeeze out as much liquid from the grated cucumber as possible or your tzatziki may end up watery.

Per serving: Calories: 114; Total fat: 9g; Total carbs: 5g; Sugar: 5g; Protein: 3g; Fiber: 0g; Sodium: 135mg

# Greek Garlic Dip | Skordalia

Serves: **4** | Prep time: **10 minutes** | Cook time: **30 minutes** | **5-Ingredient**

Fluffy mashed potatoes provide the thick base for this dip. Mixed with garlic, tart lemon juice, and olive oil, the potatoes create a smooth emulsion bursting with flavor. The combination of ingredients is a perfect middle ground between a dip and a side that pairs well with fish, meat, or vegetables.

2 potatoes (about 1 pound), peeled and quartered
½ cup olive oil

¼ cup freshly squeezed lemon juice
4 garlic cloves, minced
Sea salt

Freshly ground black pepper

1. Place the potatoes in a large saucepan and fill the pan three-quarters full with water. Bring the water to a boil over medium-high heat, then reduce the heat to medium and cook the potatoes until fork-tender, 20 to 30 minutes.

2. While the potatoes are boiling, in a medium bowl, stir together the olive oil, lemon juice, and garlic; set aside.

3. Drain the potatoes and return them to the saucepan. Pour in the oil mixture and mash with a potato masher or a fork until well combined and smooth. Taste and season with salt and pepper. Serve.

**STORAGE:** Store the dip in an airtight container in the refrigerator for up to 4 days.

**COOKING TIP:** Do not use a food processor or blender to mash the potatoes, or they will turn into a gummy mess and the dip will not taste good.

**VARIATION TIP:** You can also use day-old bread or ground nuts in place of the potatoes, and the dish would still be authentic.

Per serving: Calories: 334; Total fat: 27g; Total carbs: 22g; Sugar: 1g; Protein: 3g; Fiber: 3g; Sodium: 47mg

# Mediterranean Salad with Bulgur

Serves: **4** | Prep time: **27 minutes** | Cook time: **12 minutes** | **30-Minute**

This recipe is inspired by the Mediterranean region as a whole. It combines vegetables, whole grain, seeds, olives, and olive oil in a delightful blend of flavors and textures. Taste as you go and feel free to adjust the ingredients to your liking.

1 cup water

½ cup dried bulgur

1 (9-ounce) bag chopped romaine lettuce

1 English cucumber, cut into ¼-inch-thick slices

1 red bell pepper, chopped

½ cup raw hulled pumpkin seeds

20 kalamata olives, pitted and halved lengthwise

¼ cup extra-virgin olive oil

Juice of 1 small orange

Juice of 1 small lemon

¼ teaspoon dried oregano

Sea salt

Freshly ground black pepper

1.  In a medium saucepan, combine the water and bulgur and bring to a boil over medium heat. Reduce the heat to low, cover, and cook until the bulgur is tender, about 12 minutes. Drain off any excess liquid, fluff the bulgur with a fork, and set aside.

2.  In a medium bowl, toss together the lettuce, cucumber, bell pepper, bulgur, pumpkin seeds, and olives and set aside.

3.  In a small bowl, stir together the olive oil, orange juice, lemon juice, and oregano. Season with salt and black pepper.

4.  Add 3 tablespoons of the dressing to the salad and toss to coat. Taste, add more dressing and season with additional salt and/or black pepper if needed, then serve.

**STORAGE:** This recipe makes about ½ cup dressing, so you'll likely have some left over. Store any extra dressing in an airtight container in the refrigerator for up to 1 week.

**INGREDIENT TIP:** To save some prep time, buy precooked bulgur, available in most grocery stores.

Per serving: Calories: 322; Total fat: 23g; Total carbs: 24g; Sugar: 5g; Protein: 8g; Fiber: 6g; Sodium: 262mg

# Greek Village Salad | Horiatiki Salad

Serves: **4** | Prep time: **10 minutes** | **No-Cook** | **30-Minute**

If you have ever ordered a Greek salad at a restaurant, you undoubtedly received a version of *horiatiki*, probably bulked up with lettuce. This salad highlights the incredible taste of ripe tomatoes, bell peppers, cool cucumber, and sharp onion, and is best prepared in the summer when these vegetables are in season. You might notice that the olives are whole and the feta is left in one slice rather than crumbled. This presentation is traditional for this popular salad.

5 large tomatoes, cut into medium chunks

2 red onions, cut into medium chunks or sliced

1 English cucumber, peeled and cut into medium chunks

2 green bell peppers, cut into medium chunks

¼ cup extra-virgin olive oil, plus extra for drizzling

1 cup kalamata olives, for topping

¼ teaspoon dried oregano, plus extra for garnish

¼ lemon

4 ounces Greek feta cheese, sliced

1. In a large bowl, mix the tomatoes, onions, cucumber, bell peppers, olive oil, olives, and oregano.

2. Divide the vegetable mixture evenly among four bowls and top each with a squirt of lemon juice and 1 slice of feta. Drizzle with olive oil, garnish with oregano, and serve.

**STORAGE:** Store any leftover salad in an airtight container in the refrigerator for up to 2 days.

**INGREDIENT TIP:** For milder red onions, soak them in ice water for 10 to 20 minutes to tame their bite.

Per serving: Calories: 315; Total fat: 24g; Total carbs: 21g; Sugar: 12g; Protein: 8g; Fiber: 6g; Sodium: 524mg

# Valencia-Inspired Salad

Serves: **4** | Prep time: **15 minutes** | **No-Cook** | **30-Minute**

Valencia oranges are common in grocery stores in the summer months, when they are in season and bursting with intensely sweet, invigorating juice. Spain is famous for its citrus, but these bright oranges were created in the United States and named after the city of Valencia. This colorful salad is perfect for a summer plate.

2 small oranges, peeled, thinly sliced, and pitted

1 small blood orange, peeled, thinly sliced, and pitted

1 (7-ounce) bag butter lettuce

½ English cucumber, thinly sliced into rounds

1 (6-ounce) can pitted black olives, halved

1 small shallot, thinly sliced (optional)

¼ cup raw hulled pumpkin seeds

8 slices Manchego cheese, roughly broken

2 to 3 tablespoons extra-virgin olive oil

Juice of 1 orange

1. In a large bowl, toss together the oranges, lettuce, cucumber, olives, shallot (if desired), pumpkin seeds, and cheese until well mixed. Evenly divide the mixture among four plates.

2. Drizzle the salads with the olive oil and orange juice. Serve.

**SUBSTITUTION TIP:** You can substitute romaine lettuce for the butter lettuce and crumbled goat cheese for the Manchego.

Per serving: Calories: 419; Total fat: 31g; Total carbs: 22g; Sugar: 13g; Protein: 17g; Fiber: 5g; Sodium: 513mg

# Tabbouleh

Serves: **4 to 6 as a side** | Prep time: **15 minutes** | Cook time: **12 minutes** | **30-Minute**

This is a quick and easy version of a classic Mediterranean staple, sure to brighten any plate. Tabbouleh is a national dish of Lebanon, but variations can be found in almost every country on the Mediterranean Sea. You can put together this salad in a snap with ingredients you probably already have in the kitchen. Cooking the bulgur takes the most time, so do this ahead and store it in an airtight container in the refrigerator for up to 4 days.

1 cup water

½ cup dried bulgur

½ English cucumber, quartered lengthwise and sliced

2 tomatoes on the vine, diced

2 scallions, chopped

Juice of 1 lemon

2 cups coarsely chopped fresh Italian parsley

⅓ cup coarsely chopped fresh mint leaves

1 garlic clove

¼ cup extra-virgin olive oil

Sea salt

Freshly ground black pepper

1. In a medium saucepan, combine the water and bulgur and bring to a boil over medium heat. Reduce the heat to low, cover, and cook until the bulgur is tender, about 12 minutes. Drain off any excess liquid, fluff the bulgur with a fork, and set aside to cool.

2. In a large bowl, toss together the bulgur, cucumber, tomatoes, scallions, and lemon juice.

3. In a food processor, combine the parsley, mint, and garlic and process until finely chopped.

4. Add the chopped herb mixture to the bulgur mixture and stir to combine. Add the olive oil and stir to incorporate.

5. Season with salt and pepper and serve.

STORAGE: Store leftover tabbouleh in an airtight container in the refrigerator for up to 4 days.

VARIATION TIP: Tabbouleh is great stuffed inside cooked vegetables, like tomatoes, for a vegetarian main meal.

Per serving: Calories: 215; Total fat: 14g; Total carbs: 21g; Sugar: 3g; Protein: 4g; Fiber: 5g; Sodium: 66mg

# Italian Wedding Soup | Minestra Maritata

Serves: **5** | Prep time: **20 minutes** | Cook time: **20 minutes**

Contrary to what the name implies, this hearty soup has nothing to do with matrimony and isn't traditionally served at weddings. In this case, the word "wedding" refers to the perfect "marriage" of harmonious ingredients. This Neapolitan dish dates back to sometime around the sixteenth century and features clear and flavorful broth, dark greens, and tender meatballs. This is a hearty version of the soup from our childhoods, sure to satisfy both body and soul on a brisk day.

8 to 12 ounces ground beef

¼ cup chopped fresh Italian parsley

2 tablespoons bread crumbs

1 large egg

½ teaspoon garlic powder

½ teaspoon onion powder

2 tablespoons olive oil

1 carrot, halved lengthwise and sliced

2 celery stalks, halved lengthwise and sliced

1 shallot, chopped

½ teaspoon Italian seasoning

8 cups chicken broth

½ cup dried orzo

2 tablespoons grated Parmesan cheese

1. In a large bowl, combine the ground beef, parsley, bread crumbs, egg, garlic powder, and onion powder until well mixed. Shape the meat mixture into 1-inch meatballs and set aside on a large plate.

2. In a Dutch oven, heat the olive oil over medium-high heat. Add the carrot, celery, shallot, and Italian seasoning and sauté until softened, 3 to 5 minutes. Add the broth, cover, and bring to a boil. Add the orzo and meatballs, reduce the heat to low, and simmer, uncovered, until the meatballs are cooked through and the orzo is al dente, 10 to 15 minutes.

3. Serve topped with the Parmesan.

CONTINUES >

**STORAGE:** Store leftover soup in an airtight container in the refrigerator for up to 4 days.

**PREP TIP:** For a make-ahead meal, this recipe can easily be doubled and stored for later dinners. Use a stockpot instead of a Dutch oven to cook the soup, then let cool, transfer to airtight containers, and freeze for up to 1 month. Garnish with the Parmesan just before serving.

Per serving: Calories: 262; Total fat: 16g; Total carbs: 18g; Sugar: 4g; Protein: 12g; Fiber: 2g; Sodium: 684mg

# Fish Stew

Serves: **4 or 5** | Prep time: **15 minutes** | Cook time: **30 minutes**

The Mediterranean diet is defined by its rich and varied uses of seafood; this hearty, simple stew can be made with almost any seafood that appeals to you at the fish counter. Pancetta adds a salty richness, and the saffron-scented tomato broth calls out for a crusty heel of bread to soak up every bite.

2 tablespoons olive oil

2 ounces pancetta, cubed

2 tomatoes on the vine, diced

1 onion, chopped

1 leek, white part only, sliced and rinsed well

3 garlic cloves, minced

1 tablespoon tomato paste

Sea salt

Freshly ground black pepper

¼ teaspoon saffron threads

4 cups fish stock

2 cups water

1 russet potato, peeled and cubed

½ teaspoon red pepper flakes

1 bay leaf

2 pounds prepackaged mixed seafood or your favorite fish, cut into 1-inch chunks

1.  In a Dutch oven, heat the olive oil over medium-high heat. Add the pancetta, tomatoes, onion, leek, garlic, and tomato paste and sauté for 5 minutes. Season with salt and black pepper. Add the saffron and sauté for 30 seconds.

2.  Add the fish stock, water, potato, red pepper flakes, and bay leaf and bring the mixture to a boil. Reduce the heat to low and simmer until potato is tender, 15 to 20 minutes.

3.  Increase the heat to medium and add the fish. Simmer for 5 to 10 minutes, until the fish is cooked through. Remove the bay leaf and serve.

**STORAGE:** Store leftover stew in an airtight container in the refrigerator for up to 4 days.

**INGREDIENT TIP:** If you don't have saffron on hand, no worries—the stew will still taste delicious!

Per serving: Calories: 429; Total fat: 15g; Total carbs: 27g; Sugar: 5g; Protein: 45g; Fiber: 3g; Sodium: 836mg

# Creamy Chickpea and Tortellini Soup

Some soups are light, brothy creations, consumed to tease the appetite and perk up the taste buds. Not this Italian soup. It is a rib-sticking meal in itself, perfect for chilly autumn evenings and family get-togethers. This recipe is packed with vegetables, earthy mushrooms, chickpeas, cheesy tortellini, and cream. For a vegetarian option, just use low-sodium vegetable broth in place of the chicken broth.

2 tablespoons olive oil

1 onion, diced

3 celery stalks, chopped

4 ounces cremini (baby bella) mushrooms, quartered

6 garlic cloves, chopped

8 cups low-sodium chicken broth

2 teaspoons sea salt

1 teaspoon freshly ground black pepper

1 teaspoon Italian seasoning

¼ teaspoon paprika

10 ounces fresh spinach or cheese tortellini

1 (15-ounce) can chickpeas, drained and rinsed

3 to 4 ounces baby spinach, coarsely chopped

1 cup fresh basil, coarsely chopped

½ cup heavy (whipping) cream

1. In a Dutch oven, heat the olive oil over medium heat. Add the onion and sauté for 3 minutes. Add the celery, mushrooms, and garlic and sauté until tender, about 6 minutes. Add the broth and bring to a boil. Add the salt, pepper, Italian seasoning, and paprika and stir to combine.

2. Add the tortellini and simmer for 4 to 5 minutes (or for the amount of time recommended on the package). Add the chickpeas and simmer for 2 to 3 minutes. Add the spinach, basil, and cream. Remove from the heat and stir to combine.

3. Cover the soup and let stand for 2 minutes before serving.

**STORAGE:** Store leftover soup in an airtight container in the refrigerator for up to 4 days.

**VARIATION TIP:** Garnish each bowl with some red pepper flakes for a lovely hint of heat.

Per serving: Calories: 343; Total fat: 17g; Total carbs: 39g; Sugar: 4g; Protein: 12g; Fiber: 5g; Sodium: 614mg

# Roasted Vegetables with Lemon Tahini

Serves: **4** | Prep time: **15 minutes** | Cook time: **25 minutes**

This versatile baking sheet meal is an everyday go-to in our household. Roasting vegetables is a great way to use up anything lingering in your vegetable drawer! The tahini dressing is easy and delicious on everything. Tahini is a thick paste made from ground hulled sesame seeds (either toasted or not), and is thought to have originated in the Middle East. You can make it yourself with sesame seeds and oil in a food processor or buy it in most grocery stores.

**FOR THE DRESSING**
½ cup tahini
½ cup water, as needed
3 tablespoons freshly squeezed lemon juice
Sea salt

**FOR THE VEGETABLES**
8 ounces baby potatoes, halved

8 ounces baby carrots
1 head cauliflower, cored and cut into large chunks
2 red bell peppers, quartered
1 zucchini, cut into 1-inch pieces
¼ cup olive oil

1½ teaspoons garlic powder
¼ teaspoon dried oregano
¼ teaspoon dried thyme
Sea salt
Freshly ground black pepper
Red pepper flakes (optional)

**TO MAKE THE DRESSING**

1. In a small bowl, stir together the tahini, water, and lemon juice until well blended.

2. Taste, season with salt, and set aside.

**TO COOK THE VEGETABLES**

3. Preheat the oven to 425°F. Line a baking sheet with parchment paper.

4. Place the potatoes in a microwave-safe bowl with 3 tablespoons water, cover with a paper plate, and microwave on high for 4 minutes. Drain any excess water.

5. Transfer the potatoes to a large bowl and add the carrots, cauliflower, bell peppers, zucchini, olive oil, garlic powder, oregano, and thyme. Season with salt and black pepper.

CONTINUES >

6. Spread the vegetables in a single layer on the prepared baking sheet and roast until fork-tender and a little charred, about 25 minutes.

7. Transfer the vegetables to a large bowl and add the dressing and red pepper flakes, if desired. Toss to coat.

8. Serve the roasted vegetables alongside your favorite chicken or fish dish.

**SERVING TIP:** You can stuff the roasted vegetables into pitas for a tasty grab-and-go lunch.

Per serving: Calories: 412; Total fat: 30g; Total carbs: 31g; Sugar: 9g; Protein: 9g; Fiber: 9g; Sodium: 148mg

# Skillet Asparagus with Lemon Zest and Red Pepper Flakes

Serves: **4** | Prep time: **10 minutes** | Cook time: **10 minutes** | **5-Ingredient** | **30-Minute**

This simple preparation brings out the inherent deliciousness of asparagus. A hint of heat and some tart citrus perk up the taste buds without overpowering the flavor of this slender vegetable. When a recipe calls for lemon zest, use organic lemons whenever possible, or scrub regular lemons with a soft-bristled brush before zesting. Conventionally grown lemons are coated with a layer of wax to protect them during shipping, and you do not want to add that wax to this lovely dish.

¼ cup olive oil

2 pounds asparagus, woody ends trimmed

3 to 4 garlic cloves, minced

Zest of 1 medium lemon

¼ to ½ teaspoon red pepper flakes

Pinch sea salt, plus more as needed

Pinch freshly ground black pepper, plus more as needed

1. In a large skillet, heat the olive oil over medium-high heat. Add the asparagus and stir to coat with the oil. Sauté for 3 minutes, then add the garlic, lemon zest, red pepper flakes, salt, and black pepper and sauté for 5 to 7 minutes, until the asparagus is tender-crisp.

2. Taste and adjust the seasonings, then serve.

**SERVING TIP:** This asparagus is great served alongside your favorite lamb or fish dish.

Per serving: Calories: 171; Total fat: 14g; Total carbs: 10g; Sugar: 5g; Protein: 5g; Fiber: 5g; Sodium: 44mg

Lentil and Red Pepper Soup, *page 56*

# Beans, Rice, and Grains

# Tomato Bulgur

Serves: **4** | Prep time: **10 minutes** | Cook time: **25 minutes**

This might seem like a basic recipe when you glance through the ingredients, but the combination of sweet fresh tomatoes and tomato paste, intense paprika, and sharp lemon juice dances on the tongue. For even more flavor, it doesn't hurt to add another garlic clove or two to this nutty, healthy grain dish. We also like using roasted pine nuts as a topping for their unique flavor and pleasing crunch.

3 tablespoons olive oil

1 onion, diced

1 garlic clove, minced

1 tablespoon tomato paste

½ teaspoon paprika

3 Roma (plum) tomatoes, finely chopped, or 1 cup canned crushed tomatoes with their juices

Juice of ½ lemon

¼ teaspoon sea salt, plus more as needed

1 cup dried bulgur

2 cups vegetable broth, chicken broth, or water

1. In a large saucepan, heat the olive oil over medium-high heat. Add the onion and garlic and sauté for 4 to 5 minutes, until the onion is soft. Add the tomato paste and paprika and stir for about 30 seconds.

2. Add the chopped tomatoes, lemon juice, and salt and cook for 1 to 2 minutes more.

3. Add the bulgur and stir for about 30 seconds. Add the broth, bring to a simmer, reduce the heat to low, cover, and simmer for 13 to 15 minutes, until the liquid has been absorbed. Uncover and stir, then remove from the heat, cover, and let stand for 5 minutes.

4. Taste and adjust the seasoning, then serve.

**STORAGE:** Store leftovers in an airtight container in the refrigerator for up to 4 days.

**COOKING TIP:** There may be some water left after you've cooked the bulgur for 15 minutes, but that's okay.

Per serving: Calories: 243; Total fat: 11g; Total carbs: 34g; Sugar: 4g; Protein: 6g; Fiber: 6g; Sodium: 92mg

# Chickpea Fritters

Serves: **4 or 5** | Prep time: **15 minutes** | Cook time: **15 minutes** | 30-Minute

It's so satisfying to draw complex flavors from a humble ingredient like chickpeas. The scent of herbs and garlic will waft through your house as you fry these fritters to a perfect golden brown. These tempting little patties will remind you of falafel, so stuff them into warm pitas with shredded lettuce and a dollop of Tzatziki (page 35) for a full meal.

3 tablespoons olive oil, plus extra for frying

1 onion, chopped

2 garlic cloves, minced

1 (15-ounce) can chickpeas, drained and rinsed

1 teaspoon dried thyme

1 teaspoon dried oregano

1 teaspoon dried parsley

Sea salt

Freshly ground black pepper

¾ cup all-purpose flour, plus more as needed

1. In a large skillet, heat 1 tablespoon of the olive oil over medium-high heat. Add the onion and garlic and sauté for 5 to 7 minutes, until the onion is soft. Transfer the onion-garlic mixture to a food processor and add the remaining 2 tablespoons olive oil, the chickpeas, thyme, oregano, and parsley. Season with salt and pepper and puree until a paste forms. (If the mixture is too wet, add 1 to 2 tablespoons of flour and pulse to incorporate.)

2. Place the flour in a bowl. Scoop about 2 tablespoons of the chickpea mixture and roll it into a ball. Dredge the ball in the flour to coat, then flatten the ball slightly and place it on a plate. Repeat with the remaining chickpea mixture.

3. Wipe out the skillet and pour in 2 inches of olive oil. Heat the oil over medium-high heat. Working in batches, fry the fritters in a single layer until golden, about 3 minutes per side. Transfer them to a paper towel–lined plate. Repeat to fry the remaining fritters. Serve immediately.

**PREP TIP:** Keep your hands well floured when rolling the chickpea mixture into balls to prevent sticking.

Per serving: Calories: 290; Total fat: 12g; Total carbs: 38g; Sugar: 4g; Protein: 8g; Fiber: 6g; Sodium: 45mg

# Asparagus-Spinach Farro

Serves: **4** | Prep time: **5 minutes** | Cook time: **16 minutes** | **30-Minute**

The muted color palette of this hearty grain dish will remind you of spring, with the light brown of the farro and varying shades of green from the asparagus and spinach. Adding the asparagus at the end ensures it retains a little snap and keeps its vivid color. Be sure to buy pencil-thin asparagus, and snap off the woody ends to get the best texture. Making the farro right in the skillet ensures that it absorbs all the flavors in this dish.

2 tablespoons olive oil
1 cup quick-cooking
   farro
½ shallot, finely
   chopped
4 garlic cloves, minced
Sea salt

Freshly ground
   black pepper
2½ cups water,
   vegetable broth, or
   chicken broth

8 ounces asparagus,
   woody ends trimmed,
   cut into 2-inch pieces
3 ounces fresh baby
   spinach
½ cup grated Parmesan
   cheese

1.  In a large skillet, heat the olive oil over medium-high heat. Add the farro, shallot, and garlic, season with salt and pepper, and cook for about 4 minutes. Add the water and bring the mixture to a boil. Reduce the heat to low, cover, and simmer for 10 minutes (or for the time recommended on the package of farro).

2.  Add the asparagus and cook until tender, about 5 minutes. Add the spinach and cook for 30 seconds more, or until wilted.

3.  Top with the Parmesan and serve.

**STORAGE:** Store leftovers in an airtight container in the refrigerator for up to 4 days.

**INGREDIENT TIP:** If you can't find quick-cooking farro, use whichever type is available and adjust the cooking time as necessary (check the package for recommended cooking times).

Per serving: Calories: 277; Total fat: 11g; Total carbs: 38g; Sugar: 1g; Protein: 10g; Fiber: 7g; Sodium: 284mg

# Harissa Rice with White Beans

Serves: **4** | Prep time: **5 minutes** | Cook time: **30 minutes** | **5-Ingredient**

This simple dish makes an ideal weeknight dinner and might remind you of popular red beans and rice from the southern United States. This is a natural pairing of two staple ingredients from North Africa and other countries, and combining rice and beans creates a complete protein. The harissa adds a tint of red to the dish and, of course, contributes heat and flavor.

1 tablespoon olive oil

1 cup uncooked white rice

1 tablespoon harissa

2 garlic cloves, minced

1 (15-ounce) can great Northern beans, drained and rinsed

2 cups vegetable broth

¼ teaspoon sea salt

1. In a large stockpot, heat the olive oil over medium-high heat. Add the rice and sauté for 2 to 3 minutes. Add the harissa and garlic and sauté for 1 to 2 minutes. Add the beans and cook for 1 minute.

2. Add the broth and salt, increase the heat to high, and bring to a boil. Boil for 1 minute, then reduce the heat to low, cover, and simmer for 20 minutes, or until the liquid has been absorbed. Serve.

**STORAGE:** Store leftovers in an airtight container in the refrigerator for up to 4 days.

**VARIATION TIP:** If you'd like the rice spicier, which can be delicious, use 1½ to 2 tablespoons harissa.

Per serving: Calories: 295; Total fat: 4g; Total carbs: 55g; Sugar: 1g; Protein: 9g; Fiber: 6g; Sodium: 355mg

# Two-Bean Bulgur Chili

Serves: **4 or 5** | Prep time: **10 minutes** | Cook time: **30 minutes**

This is a Mediterranean twist on chili, an American classic, continuing the tradition of cultural culinary exchange that defines Mediterranean food. Fresh vegetables, legumes, whole grains, and warm cumin blend beautifully with chili powder and hot jalapeño pepper.

2 tablespoons olive oil
1 onion, diced
2 celery stalks, diced
1 carrot, diced
1 jalapeño pepper,
  seeded and chopped
3 garlic cloves, minced
1 (28-ounce) can
  diced tomatoes
1 tablespoon
  tomato paste

1½ teaspoons
  chili powder
2 teaspoons dried
  oregano
2 teaspoons
  ground cumin
1 (15-ounce) can
  black beans, drained
  and rinsed

1 (15-ounce) can
  cannellini beans,
  drained and rinsed
¾ cup dried bulgur
4 cups chicken broth
Sea salt
Freshly ground
  black pepper

1. In a Dutch oven, heat the olive oil over medium-high heat. Add the onion, celery, carrot, jalapeño, and garlic and sauté until the vegetables are tender, about 4 minutes.

2. Reduce the heat to medium and add the diced tomatoes, tomato paste, chili powder, oregano, and cumin. Cook for 3 minutes, then add the black beans, cannellini beans, bulgur, and broth.

3. Increase the heat to high, cover, and bring to a boil. Reduce the heat to low and simmer until the chili is cooked to your desired thickness, about 30 minutes. Season with salt and black pepper and serve.

**STORAGE:** Store leftovers in an airtight container in the refrigerator for up to 4 days or in the freezer for up to 1 month.

**SERVING TIP:** This dish would be delicious topped with sour cream, crème fraîche, onions, scallions, shredded cheese, feta cheese, or kalamata olives (or a combination of these).

Per serving: Calories: 385; Total fat: 9g; Total carbs: 64g; Sugar: 8g; Protein: 17g; Fiber: 20g; Sodium: 325mg

# Moroccan Date Pilaf

Serves: **4 or 5** | Prep time: **10 minutes** | Cook time: **30 minutes**

This dish is an ideal showcase for North African flavors, blending fruity sweetness with savory rice and a dash of heat. It's important to let this one rest for a bit after cooking so the flavors can settle. You can use any type of date in this recipe, but Medjool dates are an inspired choice because of their rich caramel flavor and yielding texture.

3 tablespoons olive oil
1 onion, chopped
3 garlic cloves, minced
1 cup uncooked
  long-grain rice
½ to 1 tablespoon
  harissa

5 or 6 Medjool dates
  (or another variety),
  pitted and chopped
¼ cup dried cranberries
¼ teaspoon ground
  cinnamon
½ teaspoon ground
  turmeric

¼ teaspoon sea salt
¼ teaspoon freshly
  ground black pepper
2 cups chicken broth
¼ cup shelled whole
  pistachios, for garnish

1. In a large stockpot, heat the olive oil over medium heat. Add the onion and garlic and sauté for 3 to 5 minutes, until the onion is soft. Add the rice and cook for 3 minutes, until the grains start to turn opaque. Add the harissa, dates, cranberries, cinnamon, turmeric, salt, and pepper and cook for 30 seconds. Add the broth and bring to a boil, then reduce the heat to low, cover, and simmer for 20 minutes, or until the liquid has been absorbed.

2. Remove the rice from the heat and stir in the nuts. Let stand for 10 minutes before serving.

**STORAGE:** Store leftovers in an airtight container in the refrigerator for up to 4 days.

**SUBSTITUTION TIP:** If you cannot find dates, dried apricots would be lovely in their place; use about 1 cup chopped dried apricots.

Per serving: Calories: 368; Total fat: 15g; Total carbs: 54g; Sugar: 13g; Protein: 6g; Fiber: 4g; Sodium: 83mg

# Lentil and Red Pepper Soup

Serves: **4** | Prep time: **15 minutes** | Cook time: **25 minutes**

This is an easy, healthy soup; adding feta cheese at the end infuses brightness into the earthy flavors. There are two kinds of lentil soup: the type that's a thick, porridgelike soup, and the type where the lentils retain their basic shape so you can see each individual one. If you like the second type, reduce the simmering time or use green lentils instead of red.

2 tablespoons olive oil

2 red bell peppers, coarsely chopped

1 onion, coarsely chopped

1¾ cups shredded carrots

2 tomatoes on the vine, coarsely chopped

5 garlic cloves, coarsely chopped

Sea salt

Freshly ground black pepper

8 cups chicken broth

2 cups dried red lentils

1 teaspoon dried oregano

½ teaspoon dried rosemary

Juice of ½ lemon

½ cup crumbled feta cheese, for serving

1.  In a large stockpot, heat the olive oil over medium-high heat. Add the bell peppers, onion, carrots, tomatoes, and garlic and stir to combine. Season with salt and black pepper and cook for 5 to 7 minutes, until the onion is soft. Add the broth, lentils, oregano, and rosemary and bring to a boil. Reduce the heat to low and simmer for 20 minutes, or until the lentils are tender.

2.  Using an immersion blender or a food processor, puree the soup until smooth. Stir in the lemon juice. Taste and adjust the seasonings, if desired.

3.  Serve topped with the feta.

**STORAGE:** Store leftovers in an airtight container in the refrigerator for up to 4 days.

**COOKING TIP:** You can coarsely chop the bell peppers, onion, tomatoes, and garlic because you'll be blending the soup before serving.

Per serving: Calories: 521; Total fat: 13g; Total carbs: 76g; Sugar: 9g; Protein: 28g; Fiber: 14g; Sodium: 258mg

# Pita Bread

Makes: **7 pitas** | Prep time: **2 hours** | Cook time: **21 minutes** | **5-Ingredient**

This is an easy shortcut to fill your house with that fresh-baked-bread smell. We make this on a weekend morning when we have some extra time, and then we enjoy fresh pita for the rest of the week. Once you get the hang of exactly when the pita puffs and what its color should be, this recipe will become second nature.

3 cups all-purpose flour, plus extra for dusting
1 cup warm water

2 tablespoons honey
2 tablespoons olive oil, plus extra for greasing

1 (¼-ounce) packet instant yeast
1½ teaspoons sea salt

1. In a large bowl, combine the flour, warm water, honey, olive oil, yeast, and salt and mix until a dough is formed. Add water a little at a time if the dough is too dry, or a little flour if the dough is too wet.

2. Turn the dough out onto a lightly floured surface and knead for 5 minutes, then form the dough into a ball.

3. Lightly oil a large bowl. Transfer the dough to the bowl, turning to coat the dough with oil. Cover the bowl with plastic wrap and set aside to rise for 1 hour 30 minutes, or until doubled in size.

4. Preheat the oven to 450°F.

5. Place the dough on a lightly floured surface and separate it into 7 equal balls. Roll out each ball into an 8-inch round. Place 2 or 3 pitas on a baking sheet, spaced apart so they do not touch, and bake for 5 to 7 minutes, until they puff up. Remove the pitas from the baking sheet and repeat with the remaining dough.

6. Serve.

STORAGE: Store leftover pitas in an airtight container in the refrigerator for up to 4 days.

Per serving: Calories: 251; Total fat: 4g; Total carbs: 46g; Sugar: 5g; Protein: 6g; Fiber: 2g; Sodium: 251mg

# Greek Yogurt Corn Bread

Serves: **4 to 6** | Prep time: **15 minutes** | Cook time: **25 minutes**

This modern take on corn bread blends flavors from the New and Old Worlds. We love drizzling a little honey over each piece; it pairs nicely with the salty feta, which is stirred directly into the batter. For an extra flavor boost, add ½ cup chopped pancetta or chopped pitted black olives along with the feta.

⅓ cup olive oil, plus extra for greasing

1 cup cornmeal

1 cup all-purpose flour

¼ cup sugar

½ teaspoon baking soda

½ teaspoon baking powder

1 teaspoon sea salt

1 cup plain full-fat Greek yogurt

1 large egg

¼ cup crumbled feta cheese

1. Preheat the oven to 375°F. Lightly grease an 8-inch square baking dish with olive oil.

2. In a large bowl, stir together the cornmeal, flour, sugar, baking soda, baking powder, and salt until well mixed. Add the yogurt, olive oil, and egg and stir until smooth. Stir in the feta.

3. Pour the batter into the prepared baking dish and bake until a toothpick inserted into the center of the corn bread comes out clean, about 30 minutes.

4. Remove the corn bread from the oven, cut it into 9 squares, and serve.

**STORAGE:** Store leftover corn bread in an airtight container in the refrigerator for up to 4 days.

**SERVING TIP:** This corn bread pairs well with Two-Bean Bulgur Chili (page 54). We sometimes like to put a small piece at the bottom of each bowl before ladling in the chili.

Per serving: Calories: 546; Total fat: 24g; Total carbs: 71g; Sugar: 16g; Protein: 11g; Fiber: 2g; Sodium: 584mg

# Chicken and Chickpea Stew

Serves: **4** | Prep time: **15 minutes** | Cook time: **30 minutes**

This is a quintessential one-pot stew. Throw together tender chicken, legumes, heaps of vegetables, and herbs and let the magic happen. Chicken drumsticks are an inspired choice because they are the most flavorful part of the bird, but thighs would also be lovely in this filling stew.

3 tablespoons olive oil

1½ pounds chicken drumsticks

1 onion, chopped

2 leeks, white parts only, chopped and rinsed well

2 red bell peppers, chopped

1 carrot, chopped

4 garlic cloves, minced

Juice of ½ lemon

2 cups chicken broth

1 (15-ounce) can diced tomatoes

1 (15-ounce) can chickpeas, drained and rinsed

½ teaspoon red pepper flakes, or more if desired

½ teaspoon dried oregano

¼ teaspoon dried sage

¼ teaspoon dried rosemary

Sea salt

Freshly ground black pepper

1. In a large stockpot, heat the olive oil over medium heat. Add the chicken and cook, turning it frequently, for 10 minutes, or until browned.

2. Add the onion, leeks, bell peppers, carrot, garlic, and lemon juice and sauté for 5 minutes. Add the broth, tomatoes, chickpeas, red pepper flakes, oregano, sage, and rosemary. Bring to a boil, reduce the heat to low, cover, and simmer for 15 to 20 minutes, until chicken is cooked through.

3. Season with salt and black pepper and serve.

**STORAGE:** Store leftover stew in an airtight container in the refrigerator for up to 4 days.

**SUBSTITUTION TIP:** This recipe works great with cannellini or any other white bean in place of the chickpeas.

Per serving: Calories: 546; Total fat: 28g; Total carbs: 35g; Sugar: 11g; Protein: 39g; Fiber: 9g; Sodium: 345mg

# Creamy Pea Soup

Serves: **4** | Prep time: **10 minutes** | Cook time: **40 minutes**

Split peas are one of the healthiest ingredients you can add to soups and other recipes. This legume is high in protein and fiber, low in calories, and an excellent source of vitamins A and B. Split peas cook faster than most other legumes, so they're a fabulous choice when you want to get a meal on the table quickly. Greek yogurt is a wonderfully healthy way to add creamy deliciousness to soups.

1 pound dried split
  green peas
2 tablespoons olive oil
1 onion,
  coarsely chopped

2 garlic cloves,
  coarsely chopped
3 cups vegetable broth
  or chicken broth

6 ounces plain full-fat
  Greek yogurt, at
  room temperature
Sea salt
Freshly ground
  black pepper

1. Place the split peas in a large stockpot and add water to cover by about 2 inches. Bring the water to a boil over high heat, reduce the heat to low, and simmer until the peas are tender, 20 to 30 minutes. Drain the peas and set aside in a medium bowl.

2. In the same stockpot, heat the olive oil over medium-high heat. Add the onion and garlic and sauté for 5 to 7 minutes, or until the onion is soft. Return the cooked peas to the pot, add the broth, and puree with an immersion blender. Cook over medium heat until heated through, about 5 minutes.

3. Add the yogurt and season with salt and pepper. Taste, adjust the seasonings, and serve.

**STORAGE:** Store leftover soup in an airtight container in the refrigerator for up to 4 days.

**PREP TIP:** If you prefer a thicker soup, add 1½ teaspoons all-purpose flour before blending.

Per serving: Calories: 513; Total fat: 10g; Total carbs: 81g; Sugar: 15g; Protein: 29g; Fiber: 30g; Sodium: 82mg

# Garlic Shrimp with Quinoa

Serves: **4** | Prep time: **10 minutes** | Cook time: **30 minutes**

Shrimp might seem like a luxury item, but it is an easy and delicious way to get protein into your weeknight meal rotation. Shrimp can be an intimidating ingredient, especially if you are trying to determine which are small, medium, or large. A quick reference is to find the "count" of the shrimp, a number or range of numbers that tells you how many shrimp you'll typically get in 1 pound; the higher the number, the smaller the shrimp.

4 cups chicken broth

2 cups uncooked quinoa, rinsed

5 tablespoons olive oil

½ red onion, chopped

6 garlic cloves, minced

1 tablespoon tomato paste

1 teaspoon chili powder

Sea salt

Freshly ground black pepper

1½ pounds medium shrimp (36/40 count), peeled and deveined

½ cup crumbled feta cheese, for garnish

1. In a large stockpot, combine the broth and quinoa and bring to a boil over high heat. Reduce the heat to low, cover, and simmer for 20 to 25 minutes, until the quinoa is cooked. Drain the quinoa and set aside in a medium bowl.

2. Rinse and dry the pot. Pour in the olive oil and heat over medium heat. Add the onion, garlic, tomato paste, and chili powder and cook for 1 minute. Season with salt and pepper and stir to combine. Add the shrimp and cook until the shrimp are pink and just cooked through, 5 to 7 minutes.

3. Return the quinoa to the pot and stir everything together. Remove from the heat.

4. Serve topped with the feta.

**STORAGE:** Store leftovers in an airtight container in the refrigerator for up to 3 days.

**SUBSTITUTION TIP:** This recipe works well with farro or bulgur in place of the quinoa.

Per serving: Calories: 650; Total fat: 28g; Total carbs: 62g; Sugar: 2g; Protein: 38g; Fiber: 7g; Sodium: 1,011mg

Linguine with Avocado Pesto, *page 70*

# Pizza and Pasta

# Classic Margherita Pizza

Serves: **4** | Prep time: **10 minutes** | Cook time: **10 minutes** | **30-Minute**

This is a classic pizza from Italy made with three ingredients representing the colors of the Italian flag: basil (green), mozzarella (white), and tomato sauce (red). Simple, yet amazingly delicious. Pick up prepared pizza dough at your local grocery store, or use your favorite pizza dough recipe instead.

All-purpose flour, for dusting

1 pound premade pizza dough

1 (15-ounce) can crushed San Marzano tomatoes, with their juices

2 garlic cloves

1 teaspoon Italian seasoning

Pinch sea salt, plus more as needed

1½ teaspoons olive oil, for drizzling

10 slices mozzarella cheese

12 to 15 fresh basil leaves

1. Preheat the oven to 475°F.

2. On a floured surface, roll out the dough to a 12-inch round and place it on a lightly floured pizza pan or baking sheet.

3. In a food processor, combine the tomatoes with their juices, garlic, Italian seasoning, and salt and process until smooth. Taste and adjust the seasoning.

4. Drizzle the olive oil over the pizza dough, then spoon the pizza sauce over the dough and spread it out evenly with the back of the spoon, leaving a 1-inch border. Evenly distribute the mozzarella over the pizza.

5. Bake until the crust is cooked through and golden, 8 to 10 minutes. Remove from the oven and let sit for 1 to 2 minutes. Top with the basil right before serving.

**STORAGE:** Store any leftover sauce and leftover pizza in separate airtight containers in the refrigerator for up to 3 days.

**COOKING TIP:** If you're working with wet mozzarella slices, let them sit between paper towels for 5 to 10 minutes to remove some of the liquid. If you skip this step, the cheese will release liquid during baking, resulting in a soggy pizza.

Per serving: Calories: 540; Total fat: 21g; Total carbs: 62g; Sugar: 11g; Protein: 27g; Fiber: 5g; Sodium: 1,094mg

# Chorizo and Manchego Pizza

Serves: **4** | Prep time: **15 minutes** | Cook time: **10 minutes** | **30-Minute**

This pizza pays homage to Spain. Manchego is a rich Spanish cheese that holds well when mixed with the other ingredients. This recipe uses thinly sliced cured chorizo, which delivers a bit of heat to each bite. The ingredient quantities are flexible, so adjust the number of garlic cloves and the amount of chorizo to your personal preference. If you are a garlic fan, add more and enjoy!

All-purpose flour, for dusting

1 pound premade pizza dough

¾ cup shredded Parmesan cheese

2 to 3 garlic cloves, minced

4 or 5 slices cured (Spanish) chorizo, coarsely chopped

½ cup grated Manchego cheese

1. Preheat the oven to 475°F.

2. On a floured surface, roll out the dough to a 12-inch round and place it on a lightly floured pizza pan or baking sheet.

3. In a small bowl, mix the Parmesan and garlic and sprinkle the mixture over the pizza dough. Top with the chorizo. Bake for 8 to 10 minutes, until the crust is cooked through and golden. Remove the pizza from the oven and turn the oven off.

4. Sprinkle the pizza evenly with the Manchego and return it to the oven (still turned off) for 1 minute to allow the Manchego to melt.

5. Remove from the oven, slice, and serve.

**STORAGE:** Store leftover pizza in an airtight container in the refrigerator for up to 3 days.

**VARIATION TIP:** For a little extra heat, top the pizza with red pepper flakes. Make sure the chorizo is cured Spanish sausage and not in a casing.

Per serving: Calories: 578; Total fat: 21g; Total carbs: 75g; Sugar: 8g; Protein: 27g; Fiber: 4g; Sodium: 1,312mg

# Chicken and Goat Cheese Pizza

Serves: **3 or 4** | Prep time: **10 minutes** | Cook time: **10 minutes** | **5-Ingredient** | **30-Minute**

Creamy goat cheese is one of our favorite ingredients, whether we're cooking a Mediterranean dish or any other type of cuisine. It goes with everything from breakfast crêpes to salads to this popular dish–pizza! This simple pizza is one we make when we have leftover cooked chicken.

All-purpose flour, for dusting

1 pound premade pizza dough

2 tablespoons olive oil

1 cup shredded cooked chicken

3 ounces goat cheese, crumbled

Sea salt

Freshly ground black pepper

1. Preheat the oven to 475°F.

2. On a floured surface, roll out the dough to a 12-inch round and place it on a lightly floured pizza pan or baking sheet. Drizzle the dough with the olive oil and spread it out evenly. Top the dough with the chicken and goat cheese.

3. Bake the pizza for 8 to 10 minutes, until the crust is cooked through and golden.

4. Season with salt and pepper and serve.

**STORAGE:** Store leftover pizza in an airtight container in the refrigerator for up to 3 days.

**VARIATION TIP:** Sprinkle the pizza with a little garlic powder or add fresh basil or chopped artichoke hearts for different flavors.

Per serving: Calories: 593; Total fat: 21g; Total carbs: 70g; Sugar: 8g; Protein: 31g; Fiber: 4g; Sodium: 924mg

# Calzone

Serves: **4** | Prep time: **15 minutes** | Cook time: **35 minutes**

Ahh, the wonderful, delicious Italian calzone. Traditionally, you'd probably find these golden baked half-moons stuffed with just ricotta and some mozzarella, served with a side of picante tomato sauce. However, it's your kitchen, so your rules—feel free to stuff these calzones with whatever you want.

1 pound premade pizza dough

All-purpose flour, for dusting

½ cup ricotta cheese

¼ cup chopped fresh Italian parsley

4 slices prosciutto

4 small bell peppers, diced

1 large egg, beaten with a splash of water, for the egg wash

1. Preheat the oven to 375°F. Line a baking sheet with parchment paper.

2. Divide the pizza dough into 2 equal pieces and roll them out on a lightly floured surface into two 10-inch rounds.

3. In a small bowl, combine the ricotta and parsley and evenly divide the mixture between the dough rounds. Spread the ricotta over one half of each dough round, leaving a 1-inch border on the outside edge. Top the ricotta with the prosciutto and bell peppers. Fold the dough over to create a half-moon shape and pinch the edges together to seal. Fold the sealed seam over and crimp the edge with the tines of a fork.

4. Place the calzones on the prepared baking sheet, brush them with the egg wash, and bake for about 35 minutes, until golden brown.

5. Serve with pizza sauce or whatever you like!

**STORAGE:** Store leftovers in an airtight container in the refrigerator for up to 3 days.

**VARIATION TIP:** This recipe makes two large calzones that are meant to be shared, so adjust accordingly. Remember, the more filling you add, the bigger they get. Some suggestions for other fillings include mushrooms and artichoke hearts.

Per serving: Calories: 395; Total fat: 10g; Total carbs: 58g; Sugar: 9g; Protein: 20g; Fiber: 5g; Sodium: 794mg

# Mediterranean Pasta Salad

Serves: **4** | Prep time: **20 minutes** | Cook time: **15 minutes**

This simple, healthy pasta salad can be served as either a main or a side. It goes well with almost anything and is packed with legumes, vegetables, and dark leafy greens, so it's filling enough to be served on its own. The feta cheese really brings the dish together.

4 cups dried farfalle (bow-tie) pasta

1 cup canned chickpeas, drained and rinsed

⅔ cup water-packed artichoke hearts, drained and diced

½ red onion, thinly sliced

1 cup packed baby spinach

½ red bell pepper, diced

1 Roma (plum) tomato, diced

½ English cucumber, quartered lengthwise and cut into ½-inch pieces

⅓ cup extra-virgin olive oil

Juice of ½ lemon

Sea salt

Freshly ground black pepper

½ cup crumbled feta cheese

1. Fill a large saucepan three-quarters full with water and bring to a boil over high heat. Add the pasta and cook according to the package directions until al dente, about 15 minutes. Drain the pasta and run it under cold water to stop the cooking process and cool.

2. While the pasta is cooking, in a large bowl, mix the chickpeas, artichoke hearts, onion, spinach, bell pepper, tomato, and cucumber.

3. Add the pasta to the bowl with the vegetables. Add the olive oil and lemon juice and season with salt and black pepper. Mix well.

4. Top the salad with the feta and serve.

**STORAGE:** Store leftovers in an airtight container in the refrigerator for up to 4 days.

**COOKING TIP:** The quality of your extra-virgin olive oil will make or break this dish, so make sure you get a premium EVOO. Regular olive oil won't provide the necessary flavor.

Per serving: Calories: 702; Total fat: 25g; Total carbs: 99g; Sugar: 8g; Protein: 22g; Fiber: 10g; Sodium: 207mg

# Spaghetti with Clams | Spaghetti alle Vongole

Serves: **4** | Prep time: **5 minutes** | Cook time: **10 minutes** | **30-Minute**

This spaghetti and clams dish is a staple of Southern Italy. The simplicity of the ingredients and clean flavors create a sublime dish. Briny clams, garlic, red pepper flakes, and gorgeous green parsley are accented by a lovely buttery sauce. This classic dish pairs well with a nice glass of crisp white wine and some warm crusty bread.

1 pound dried spaghetti
¼ cup olive oil
2 tablespoons unsalted butter
4 garlic cloves, minced

1 (12-ounce) can minced clams, with their juices
½ teaspoon red pepper flakes

¼ cup chopped fresh Italian parsley
Freshly ground black pepper

1. Fill a large stockpot three-quarters full with water and bring to a boil over high heat. Add the pasta and cook according to the package instructions until al dente, about 15 minutes. Drain and set aside.

2. In the same stockpot, heat the olive oil and butter over medium-high heat. Add the garlic and sauté until fragrant, 3 to 4 minutes. Add the clams and their juices and the red pepper flakes and cook for 2 to 3 minutes. Remove from the heat, add the spaghetti, and toss to combine.

3. Serve topped with the parsley and seasoned with black pepper.

COOKING TIP: Add some grated Parmesan cheese when you combine the spaghetti with the sauce. You can also add a splash of white wine with the clams.

Per serving: Calories: 697; Total fat: 22g; Total carbs: 90g; Sugar: 3g; Protein: 32g; Fiber: 4g; Sodium: 135mg

# Linguine with Avocado Pesto

Serves: **4** | Prep time: **10 minutes** | Cook time: **10 minutes** | **30-Minute**

Avocado pesto is our favorite condiment, and we make this dish often. The avocados give the pesto a creamy texture that perfectly coats the linguine to create a delicious bite every time. Choose ripe avocados if you plan to make this pesto immediately, or buy firmer ones and let them ripen in a paper bag on your counter to use later in the week. A ripe avocado should feel soft but not mushy when cupped in your hand and should yield a little to pressure.

1 pound dried linguine

2 avocados, coarsely chopped

½ cup olive oil

½ cup packed fresh basil

½ cup pine nuts

Juice of 1 lemon

3 garlic cloves

1 tablespoon packed sun-dried tomatoes

⅛ teaspoon Italian seasoning

⅛ teaspoon red pepper flakes

Sea salt

Freshly ground black pepper

1. Fill a large stockpot three-quarters full with water and bring to a boil over high heat. Add the pasta and cook according to the package instructions until al dente, about 15 minutes.

2. While the pasta is cooking, in a food processor, combine the avocados, olive oil, basil, pine nuts, lemon juice, garlic, sun-dried tomatoes, Italian seasoning, and red pepper flakes and process until a paste forms. Taste and season with salt and black pepper.

3. When the pasta is done, drain it and return it to the pot. Add half the pesto and mix. Add more pesto as desired and serve.

**STORAGE:** Store leftover pesto in an airtight container in the refrigerator for up to 4 days and any leftover pasta in a separate airtight container for up to 3 days.

**VARIATION TIP:** This pesto is perfect for spreading on bread, as a dip for vegetables, and even for topping chicken.

Per serving: Calories: 694; Total fat: 29g; Total carbs: 93g; Sugar: 6g; Protein: 17g; Fiber: 8g; Sodium: 11mg

# Stuffed Jumbo Pasta Shells

Serves: **4** | Prep time: **20 minutes** | Cook time: **15 minutes**

This is a fun way to serve large pasta shells. The veggie mixture delivers a tasty flavor profile, and the shells are the perfect vehicle for transporting a healthy bite. This vegetarian dish is served cold, so it is the ideal choice for a summer picnic or as a stunning potluck offering for a neighborhood or family party.

12 dried jumbo
  pasta shells
½ English cucumber,
  diced
½ cup chopped
  baby arugula
½ avocado, chopped

12 kalamata olives,
  pitted and chopped
½ cup crumbled
  feta cheese
⅓ teaspoon chopped
  fresh thyme
¼ cup olive oil

2 tablespoons freshly
  squeezed lemon juice
1 garlic clove, minced
1 teaspoon honey
Sea salt
Freshly ground
  black pepper

1. Fill a large stockpot three-quarters full with water and bring to a boil over high heat. Add the shells and cook according to the package instructions until al dente, about 15 minutes. Drain the shells and set aside to cool.

2. In a large bowl, mix the cucumber, arugula, avocado, olives, feta, and thyme.

3. In a small bowl, blend together the olive oil, lemon juice, garlic, and honey. Season with salt and pepper. Pour the dressing over the vegetables and mix well. Taste and adjust the seasonings.

4. Spoon the vegetable mixture into the shells and serve.

**SERVING TIP:** The filling can be made ahead and stored in an airtight container in the refrigerator for up to 3 days. Then just cook and stuff the shells when you're ready to serve them!

Per serving: Calories: 554; Total fat: 24g; Total carbs: 70g; Sugar: 6g; Protein: 15g; Fiber: 5g; Sodium: 306mg

# Shrimp with Angel Hair Pasta

Serves: **4 or 5** | Prep time: **10 minutes** | Cook time: **5 minutes** | **5-Ingredient** | **30-Minute**

There's something so timeless about the simplicity of this dish. Sure, you could add white wine and butter to mix things up, but olive oil, garlic, and tart lemon zest are all the flavors you need to complement the tender pink shrimp. Sometimes, simple dishes win our hearts, and we cook them again and again to celebrate their fresh ingredients.

1 pound dried angel hair pasta

2 tablespoons olive oil

3 garlic cloves, minced

1 pound large shrimp, peeled and deveined

Zest of ½ lemon

¼ cup chopped fresh Italian parsley

¼ teaspoon red pepper flakes (optional)

1. Fill a large stockpot three-quarters full with water and bring to a boil over high heat. Add the pasta and cook according to the package instructions until al dente, about 5 minutes. Drain the pasta and set aside.

2. In the same pot, heat the olive oil over medium heat. Add the garlic and sauté until fragrant, about 3 minutes. Add the shrimp and cook for about 2 minutes on each side, until pink and fully cooked.

3. Turn off the heat and return the pasta to the pot. Add the lemon zest and mix well.

4. Serve garnished with the parsley and red pepper flakes, if desired.

**STORAGE:** Store leftovers in an airtight container in the refrigerator for up to 4 days.

**INGREDIENT TIP:** A bit of heat really brings this dish together, but if you're not a fan of spice, leave out the red pepper flakes.

Per serving: Calories: 567; Total fat: 10g; Total carbs: 87g; Sugar: 3g; Protein: 31g; Fiber: 4g; Sodium: 651mg

# Spaghetti with Garlic and Oil | Spaghetti Aglio e Olio

Serves: **4 or 5** | Prep time: **10 minutes** | Cook time: **15 minutes** | **5-Ingredient** | **30-Minute**

Oddly enough, we first tried this recipe while traveling around Romania, not Italy. We instantly fell in love with the roasted garlic flavor that infuses the dish and immediately had to research all there was to know about this amazingly simple meal. It is perfect on its own or can be jazzed up with whatever ingredients you have on hand, like chicken or vegetables. This is sure to be a new Mediterranean staple in your household.

1 pound dried spaghetti
½ cup olive oil
6 garlic cloves, thinly
 sliced

¼ cup chopped fresh
 Italian parsley, plus
 more for garnish
4 tablespoons
 grated Parmesan
 cheese, divided

¼ teaspoon red
 pepper flakes
Sea salt
Freshly ground
 black pepper

1. Fill a large stockpot three-quarters full with water and bring to a boil over high heat. Add the pasta and cook according to the package instructions until al dente, about 15 minutes. Drain the pasta and set aside.

2. In the same stockpot, heat the olive oil over low heat. Add the garlic and sauté for 3 to 5 minutes, until it starts to turn a beautiful golden color. Remove the stockpot from the heat and add the cooked pasta. Toss until the pasta is coated with the olive oil and garlic.

3. Stir in the parsley, 2 tablespoons of Parmesan, and the red pepper flakes and season with salt and black pepper.

4. Divide the pasta among four bowls and top evenly with the remaining 2 tablespoons of Parmesan, then serve.

SUBSTITUTION TIP: Any long pasta shapes will work here, such as angel hair, linguine, or fettuccine. Just adjust the cooking time as indicated on the package for a perfect al dente texture.

Per serving: Calories: 694; Total fat: 31g; Total carbs: 87g; Sugar: 3g; Protein: 17g; Fiber: 4g; Sodium: 162mg

# Chicken Harissa Couscous

Serves: **4** | Prep time: **10 minutes** | Cook time: **15 minutes** | **30-Minute**

Couscous + harissa = a match made in heaven. Throw in some tender chicken, and you're off to the races. The flavor profile here is so satisfying and tasty. The couscous absorbs a hint of heat from the harissa and delivers it in every bite. This is a quick meal you will finish to the last couscous granule.

2 tablespoons olive oil
1 pound boneless, skinless chicken thighs, cut into 1-inch chunks
1 shallot, chopped
2 garlic cloves, minced

Sea salt
Freshly ground black pepper
1 teaspoon harissa
1½ cups water
1 cup dried couscous
Juice of 1 lemon

¼ cup crumbled feta cheese
¼ cup sliced almonds
¼ cup chopped fresh Italian parsley

1. In a sauté pan, heat the olive oil over medium heat. Add the chicken and sauté until just cooked through, about 8 minutes. Add the shallot and garlic and sauté for 3 minutes. Season with salt and pepper and stir in the harissa; cook for about 15 seconds.

2. Add the water, increase the heat to high, and bring to a boil. Add the couscous, stir, and remove the pan from the heat. Cover and let stand for 5 minutes.

3. Stir in the lemon juice and top with the feta. Garnish with the almonds and parsley, then serve.

**STORAGE:** Store leftovers in an airtight container in the refrigerator for up to 4 days.

**INGREDIENT TIP:** Harissa is a delicious spicy paste from Tunisia. Your local Trader Joe's should have it stocked, and other local chains may sell it in their international section. A little goes a long way, so it's a worthy purchase.

Per serving: Calories: 539; Total fat: 31g; Total carbs: 37g; Sugar: 1g; Protein: 27g; Fiber: 3g; Sodium: 224mg

# Fig Couscous

Serves: **5** | Prep time: **10 minutes** | Cook time: **10 minutes** | **30-Minute**

If couscous is not on your list of staple ingredients, it soon will be, because nothing cooks faster or soaks up more flavor than these tiny little balls. Couscous might look like a grain, but it is a pasta made from semolina. It is purchased dried and then rehydrated with boiling liquid. This dish is a delicious blend of sweet and savory that will quickly become a regular in your dinner rotation.

1½ tablespoons olive oil
¼ cup chopped onion
1 garlic clove, minced
1 teaspoon sea salt
2¾ cups chicken broth
1½ cups dried couscous

1½ cups dried figs, thinly sliced
¼ cup baby spinach
1 teaspoon ground cinnamon

¼ teaspoon ground allspice
¼ cup crumbled feta cheese (optional)

1. In a saucepan, heat the olive oil over medium heat. Add the onion, garlic, and salt and sauté until softened, about 5 minutes.

2. Add the broth and bring the mixture to a boil.

3. Remove the saucepan from the heat and stir in the couscous, figs, spinach, cinnamon, and allspice. Cover and let stand until the water has been absorbed, about 10 minutes.

4. Serve topped with the feta, if desired.

**STORAGE:** Store leftovers in an airtight container in the refrigerator for up to 4 days.

**SUBSTITUTION TIP:** If you cannot find figs in your local store, pitted dates or dried apricots make a delicious substitute.

Per serving: Calories: 348; Total fat: 5g; Total carbs: 70g; Sugar: 22g; Protein: 8g; Fiber: 8g; Sodium: 244mg

**Vegetable Tagine,** *page 83*

# CHAPTER SIX

# Vegetable Mains

# Avocado Pesto and Ricotta Flatbread with Fresh Vegetables

Serves: **4** | Prep time: **15 minutes** | Cook time: **5 minutes** | **30-Minute**

This crispy flatbread topped with our homemade avocado pesto, ricotta, and fresh vegetables is one of our favorite dishes to serve for lunch or dinner. You can have a meal on the table in less than 30 minutes, and walk away satisfied and delighted. Simple. Healthy. Delicious.

1¼ cups ricotta cheese
¼ teaspoon garlic powder
⅛ teaspoon dried oregano
⅛ teaspoon chili powder (optional)
Sea salt

Freshly ground black pepper
4 pita breads
1 batch Avocado Pesto (page 70)
1 English cucumber, thinly sliced

2 Roma (plum) tomatoes, chopped
½ red bell pepper, thinly sliced
1 tablespoon olive oil
Juice of ½ lemon

1. Heat a grill to medium-high.

2. In a small bowl, stir together the ricotta, garlic powder, oregano, and chili powder, if desired. Season with salt and black pepper.

3. Grill the pitas until lightly toasted, about 1 minute per side. Evenly divide the ricotta mixture among the warm pitas, spreading it evenly. Spread the pesto over the ricotta.

4. In a medium bowl, toss together the cucumber, tomatoes, bell pepper, olive oil, and lemon juice.

5. Top the pitas with the vegetable mixture and serve.

**COOKING TIP:** If you do not have a grill, preheat the oven to 400°F and toast the pitas on a baking sheet until lightly toasted on both sides, 3 to 5 minutes.

Per serving: Calories: 450; Total fat: 32g; Total carbs: 30g; Sugar: 5g; Protein: 14g; Fiber: 6g; Sodium: 264mg

# Veggie Mediterranean Flatbread

Serves: **4** | Prep time: **15 minutes** | Cook time: **5 minutes** | **30-Minute**

As with many other Mediterranean dishes, this recipe can be transformed into many variations depending on the vegetables you have on hand. Feel free to mix and match ingredients such as asparagus, zucchini, artichoke hearts, mushrooms, or even figs or peaches to create unique combinations.

4 flatbreads

1 large tomato, diced

1 red bell pepper, chopped

¾ cup chopped cucumber

¼ cup pitted kalamata olives, chopped

2 tablespoons olive oil

1 garlic clove, minced

¼ cup crumbled feta cheese, divided

Sea salt

Freshly ground black pepper

Juice of ½ lemon (optional)

1. Preheat the oven to 425°F.

2. Place the flatbreads on a baking sheet and bake for 5 to 7 minutes, until lightly browned and crisp.

3. While the flatbreads are baking, in a medium bowl, mix the tomato, bell pepper, cucumber, olives, olive oil, garlic, and 2 tablespoons of feta. Season with salt and black pepper.

4. Once the flatbreads are ready, remove them from the oven and let cool for a few minutes.

5. Spread the vegetable mixture over each flatbread and sprinkle with the remaining 2 tablespoons of feta and a squirt of lemon juice, if desired. Serve.

**INGREDIENT TIP:** The flatbreads can be naan, pita, or even focaccia, depending on your preference.

Per serving: Calories: 257; Total fat: 14g; Total carbs: 26g; Sugar: 4g; Protein: 7g; Fiber: 3g; Sodium: 510mg

# Stuffed Peppers with Tabbouleh

Serves: **4** | Prep time: **5 minutes** | **No-Cook** | **5-Ingredient** | **30-Minute**

We love munching on mini sweet peppers as a snack. We usually dip them in hummus, but when we saw a bowl of tabbouleh in the refrigerator one day, we thought, "Hmmm, let's stuff that colorful salad into these peppers to create a delicious crunchy bite." The fresh, tasty flavor profile is perfect for a healthy meal served with a slice of warm bread or pita.

1 pound mini
   sweet peppers

1 batch Tabbouleh
   (page 40)

Cut off the tops of the peppers and halve them lengthwise. Remove the seeds. Spoon the tabbouleh into the peppers and serve.

**STORAGE:** Store any leftover stuffed peppers in an airtight container in the refrigerator for up to 4 days.

**VARIATION TIP:** This is probably the simplest light dinner. Feel free to stuff the tabbouleh into other vegetables, but be aware that harder vegetables may need some time in the oven beforehand.

Per serving: Calories: 227; Total fat: 15g; Total carbs: 23g; Sugar: 2g; Protein: 4g; Fiber: 5g; Sodium: 466mg

# Spicy Grilled Veggie Pita

Serves: **4** | Prep time: **10 minutes** | Cook time: **15 minutes** | **30-Minute**

The star here is the harissa, a condiment that can always be found in our refrigerator. Once we discovered this red pepper paste, we never looked back. Harissa brings a delectable heat to any dish, and in this simple veggie pita sandwich, it's perfection.

4 pita breads

2 tablespoons olive oil

2 garlic cloves, minced

1 zucchini, sliced

1 red bell pepper, cut
  into strips

½ red onion, sliced

½ cup plain full-fat
  Greek yogurt or
  Hummus (page 34)

1 teaspoon harissa

1 large tomato, sliced

Sea salt

Freshly ground
  black pepper

1. Toast the pitas in a skillet over medium-high heat for 3 to 4 minutes per side, then remove from the heat and set aside.

2. In the same skillet, combine the olive oil and garlic and sauté over medium-high heat for 2 minutes. Add the zucchini, bell pepper, and onion and sauté for 5 to 6 minutes, until softened. Remove from the heat.

3. While the vegetables are cooking, in a small bowl, mix the yogurt and harissa.

4. Halve the pitas crosswise and open each half to form a pocket. Add 1 tablespoon of the yogurt mixture to each pita pocket and spread it over the inside. Spoon the cooked vegetable mixture into the pockets and top with the tomatoes. Season with salt and black pepper.

5. Serve the pitas with the extra sauce on the side.

INGREDIENT TIP: Both Greek yogurt and hummus work beautifully in these pockets. If you like heat, mix the harissa with olive oil and coat the vegetables with the mixture before adding everything to the pita.

Per serving: Calories: 215; Total fat: 10g; Total carbs: 27g; Sugar: 3g; Protein: 5g; Fiber: 5g; Sodium: 244mg

# Greek Bean Soup | Fassolatha

Serves: **4** | Prep time: **10 minutes** | Cook time: **45 minutes**

Some say this is the national dish of Greece, and in some parts of the country, there are competitions to determine the best recipe. This simple, healthy, and delicious bean soup will warm you on a cold day and keep you full. The soup is vegan, but if you don't follow a vegan diet, try adding a sprinkle of feta when you serve it.

2 tablespoons olive oil

1 large onion, chopped

1 (15-ounce) can diced tomatoes

1 (15-ounce) can great Northern beans, drained and rinsed

2 celery stalks, chopped

2 carrots, cut into long ribbons

⅓ teaspoon chopped fresh thyme

¼ cup chopped fresh Italian parsley

1 bay leaf

Sea salt

Freshly ground black pepper

1. In a Dutch oven, heat the olive oil over medium-high heat. Add the onion and sauté for 4 minutes, or until softened. Add the tomatoes, beans, celery, carrots, thyme, parsley, and bay leaf, then add water to cover by about 2 inches.

2. Bring the soup to a boil, reduce the heat to low, cover, and simmer for 30 minutes, or until the vegetables are tender.

3. Remove the bay leaf, season with salt and pepper, and serve.

**STORAGE:** Store leftovers in an airtight container in the refrigerator for up to 4 days.

**COOKING TIP:** You may need to add more water during the cooking process; for more flavor, use vegetable broth or chicken broth instead.

Per serving: Calories: 185; Total fat: 7g; Total carbs: 25g; Sugar: 6g; Protein: 7g; Fiber: 8g; Sodium: 155mg

# Vegetable Tagine

Serves: **4** | Prep time: **15 minutes** | Cook time: **45 minutes**

In North African cooking, tagines tend to be a mix of vegetables (or meat), fruit, and spices, but the word "tagine" refers to both the dish and the vessel in which it is cooked. A traditional tagine is a clay or ceramic pot with a cone-shaped lid that traps and condenses liquid that evaporates from the ingredients so you don't lose a single delicious drop. Using a stockpot with a lid mimics this process. This recipe is a winning combination that surprises many diners and keeps them coming back for more.

3 tablespoons olive oil

1 onion, thinly sliced

5 garlic cloves, minced

2 carrots, cut into long ribbons

2 red bell peppers, coarsely chopped

1 (15-ounce) can diced tomatoes

½ cup chopped dried apricots

1 to 2 tablespoons harissa

1 teaspoon ground coriander

½ teaspoon ground turmeric

½ teaspoon ground cinnamon

3 cups vegetable broth

1 sweet potato, peeled and cubed

1 (15-ounce) can chickpeas, drained and rinsed

Sea salt

Freshly ground black pepper

1. In a large stockpot, heat the olive oil over medium-high heat. Add the onion and garlic and sauté for 5 minutes. Add the carrots and bell peppers and sauté for 7 to 10 minutes, until the vegetables are tender.

2. Add the tomatoes, apricots, harissa, coriander, turmeric, and cinnamon and cook for 5 minutes. Add the broth and sweet potato and bring to a boil. Reduce the heat to low, cover, and simmer for 20 minutes, or until the sweet potato is tender.

3. Add the chickpeas and simmer for 3 minutes to heat through. Season with salt and black pepper and serve.

**STORAGE:** Store leftovers in an airtight container in the refrigerator for up to 4 days.

**SUBSTITUTION TIP:** Feel free to change up the vegetables. This tagine is a delicious way to clear out any produce left in your refrigerator.

Per serving: Calories: 324; Total fat: 12g; Total carbs: 48g; Sugar: 21g; Protein: 9g; Fiber: 12g; Sodium: 210mg

# Gnocchi with Chickpeas

Serves: **4** | Prep time: **15 minutes** | Cook time: **25 minutes**

We love making Italian gnocchi in a skillet, which creates a lovely texture that goes perfectly with the many vegetables in the dish. Feel free to add or change the vegetables to use whatever you have on hand. As with anything topped with cheese, try not to devour this dish too quickly.

4 tablespoons olive oil, divided, plus extra for drizzling

1 pound store-bought gnocchi

2 yellow squash, halved lengthwise and cut into 1-inch pieces

1 red bell pepper, diced

1 (15-ounce) can artichoke hearts, drained and chopped

½ teaspoon Italian seasoning

1 (15-ounce) can chickpeas, drained and rinsed

2 cups packed arugula

Sea salt

Freshly ground black pepper

½ cup grated Parmesan cheese, plus extra for serving

1. In a large skillet, heat 2 tablespoons of olive oil over medium-high heat. Add the gnocchi and sauté for 10 to 15 minutes, until golden brown. Remove the gnocchi from the skillet with a slotted spoon and set aside in a medium bowl.

2. In the same skillet, heat the remaining 2 tablespoons of olive oil over medium-high heat. Add the squash, bell pepper, artichoke hearts, and Italian seasoning and sauté for 10 to 12 minutes, until the vegetables are softened. Add the chickpeas and cook for 2 minutes more. Add the arugula and cook for 30 seconds, stirring to combine.

3. Return the gnocchi to the skillet and toss to mix everything together. Drizzle with olive oil, season with salt and black pepper, and top with the Parmesan. Cover with a lid and turn off the heat. Let the mixture sit for 2 minutes, or until the cheese has melted.

4. Taste and adjust the seasoning. Serve topped with extra Parmesan.

**STORAGE:** Store leftovers in an airtight container in the refrigerator for up to 4 days.

**COOKING TIP:** You can boil the gnocchi instead of sautéing it. Just prepare it according to package directions, drain, and set aside until after you've added the arugula to the pan. Adding some butter and sage to the pan before incorporating the gnocchi makes a delicious variation.

Per serving: Calories: 496; Total fat: 26g; Total carbs: 54g; Sugar: 9g; Protein: 16g; Fiber: 15g; Sodium: 553mg

# Cauliflower Steaks with Creamy Tahini Sauce

Serves: **4** | Prep time: **10 minutes** | Cook time: **40 minutes** | **5-Ingredient**

Cauliflower steaks are popular among vegetarians because of their meaty texture and ability to soak up whatever flavors are added. Here we top lightly browned, tender slabs of cauliflower with lemon tahini to bring everything together. The fresh parsley garnish is the perfect burst of color to finish the dish.

¼ cup olive oil

4 garlic cloves, minced

1 teaspoon sea salt

1 teaspoon freshly ground black pepper

2 large heads cauliflower, stem end trimmed (core left intact) and cut from top to bottom into thick slabs

½ cup tahini

Juice of 1 lemon

¼ cup chopped fresh Italian parsley

1. Preheat the oven to 400°F. Line a baking sheet with parchment paper.

2. In a small bowl, combine the olive oil, garlic, salt, and pepper. Brush this mixture on both sides of the cauliflower steaks and place them in a single layer on the baking sheet. Drizzle any remaining oil mixture over the cauliflower steaks. Bake for 45 minutes, or until the cauliflower is soft.

3. While the steaks are baking, in a small bowl, stir together the tahini and lemon juice. Season with salt and pepper.

4. Remove the cauliflower steaks from the oven and transfer them to four plates. Drizzle the lemon tahini sauce evenly over the cauliflower and garnish with the parsley. Serve.

**STORAGE:** Store leftovers in an airtight container in the refrigerator for up to 2 days.

**INGREDIENT TIP:** Whisk a tablespoon or two of water into the lemon tahini sauce if you'd like it to be thinner and easier to drizzle.

Per serving: Calories: 339; Total fat: 30g; Total carbs: 15g; Sugar: 3g; Protein: 8g; Fiber: 6g; Sodium: 368mg

# Vegetarian Pockets

Serves: **4** | Prep time: **15 minutes** | Cook time: **10 minutes** | **30-Minute**

What we love about this recipe is you can incorporate any vegetables you want, because the flavors of the tzatziki and the warm pita work with everything. Try haricots verts, asparagus, shredded carrots or parsnips, dark leafy greens, or even earthy mushrooms to create different flavor profiles.

4 pita breads

2 tablespoons olive oil

1 (15-ounce) can chickpeas, drained and rinsed

3 red bell peppers, thinly sliced

1 onion, cut into strips

1 jalapeño pepper, seeded and chopped

2 garlic cloves, minced

1 batch Tzatziki (page 35)

1. Toast the pitas in a large skillet over medium-high heat, turning them once, for about 6 minutes total. Remove from the skillet and set aside.

2. In the same skillet, heat the olive oil over medium-high heat. Add the chickpeas, bell peppers, onion, jalapeño, and garlic. Cook, stirring occasionally, for about 7 minutes, until the vegetables are tender. Remove from the heat.

3. Halve the pitas crosswise and open them to form a pocket. Spoon the chickpea-vegetable mixture into the pitas and top with the tzatziki. Serve.

**COOKING TIP:** The pitas can be grilled to create a lovely, lightly charred appearance. Grill them for about 2 minutes total, flipping them once halfway through.

Per serving: Calories: 317; Total fat: 11g; Total carbs: 45g; Sugar: 14g; Protein: 11g; Fiber: 9g; Sodium: 298mg

# Open-Faced Chickpea Salad Sandwich

Serves: **4** | Prep time: **15 minutes** | **No-Cook** | **30-Minute**

This open-faced sandwich will hit the spot, and you get twice as much filling because the bread slices are not put together. The sweet red grapes pop with flavor, and the tangy vegetables mixed with the almonds deliver the perfect crunch. Sourdough bread is our first choice because of its satisfying tangy flavor, but a crusty Italian loaf would also be delicious.

1 (15-ounce) can chickpeas, drained and rinsed

8 ounces red seedless grapes (20 to 25 grapes), halved, or quartered if large

2 celery stalks, thinly sliced

2 scallions, green part only, thinly sliced

½ red onion, chopped

¼ cup sliced almonds

¼ cup crème fraîche or mayonnaise

Juice of ½ lemon

1 tablespoon chopped fresh dill

½ teaspoon honey Dijon mustard

Sea salt

Freshly ground black pepper

8 slices sourdough bread

1. In a medium bowl, mash the chickpeas with a fork or potato masher. Stir in the grapes, celery, scallions, onion, almonds, crème fraîche, lemon juice, dill, and mustard. Season with salt and pepper.

2. Toast the bread in a toaster, then spoon the chickpea mixture onto each slice, using about ¼ cup per slice and spreading it to the edges. Serve.

**STORAGE:** Store any leftover filling in an airtight container in the refrigerator for up to 4 days; toast the bread and assemble the sandwiches just before serving.

**SERVING TIP:** This is an excellent recipe for a packed work lunch or even a picnic. You can enjoy the salad on its own or on sourdough bread as a more traditional sandwich.

Per serving: Calories: 451; Total fat: 16g; Total carbs: 64g; Sugar: 16g; Protein: 14g; Fiber: 8g; Sodium: 532mg

# Vegetarian Skillet Lasagna

Serves: **4** | Prep time: **20 minutes** | Cook time: **45 minutes**

What we love about this take on vegetable lasagna is its versatility. As with many other Mediterranean diet recipes, you can change the vegetables, using what you have on hand or need to clear out of your refrigerator. Traditionally, you wouldn't break up the noodles, so it is okay if you don't want to do it. We just thought it was a fun, creative spin on the classic method of making this dish.

15 ounces ricotta cheese

¼ cup chopped fresh Italian parsley

¼ teaspoon Italian seasoning

3 tablespoons olive oil

1 onion, coarsely chopped

3 garlic cloves, minced

2 yellow squash, quartered lengthwise and sliced into 1-inch pieces

8 ounces cremini (baby bella) mushrooms, quartered

1 carrot, cut into long ribbons

6 ounces baby spinach

1 (28-ounce) can crushed tomatoes

1½ cups heavy (whipping) cream

Sea salt

Freshly ground black pepper

9 no-bake lasagna noodles, broken into 2-inch pieces

1 cup grated Parmesan cheese

½ cup shredded mozzarella cheese

1. Preheat the oven to 375°F.

2. In a medium bowl, stir together the ricotta, parsley, and Italian seasoning and set aside.

3. In a large oven-safe skillet, heat the olive oil over medium-high heat. Add the onion and garlic and sauté for 3 minutes. Add the squash and sauté for 2 minutes more. Add the mushrooms and sauté for 4 minutes. Add the carrot and spinach and sauté for 1 minute.

CONTINUES >

4. Add the crushed tomatoes and the cream and season with salt and pepper. Add the lasagna noodles and mix well, making sure all the noodles are entirely covered with the sauce. Dollop the ricotta mixture evenly over the tomato mixture, using the back of a spoon to gently spread it around. Evenly top with the Parmesan and mozzarella. Cover the skillet with a lid and transfer it to the oven. Bake for 20 minutes, then remove the lid and bake for 10 to 15 minutes more, until the cheese is golden brown.

5. Remove from the oven and serve.

STORAGE: Store leftover lasagna in an airtight container in the refrigerator for up to 4 days.

Per serving: Calories: 1,026; Total fat: 69g; Total carbs: 71g; Sugar: 21g; Protein: 37g; Fiber: 9g; Sodium: 933mg

# Cheesy Polenta

Serves: **4** | Prep time: **10 minutes** | Cook time: **20 minutes** | **30-Minute**

This quick recipe is fabulous when you have premade polenta tubes and are looking for something to do with them. The cheesy goodness is strong here thanks to two kinds of cheese. If you cook the onions long enough, they deliver a subtle hint of sweetness.

2 tablespoons olive oil, divided

1 tablespoon unsalted butter

8 ounces cremini (baby bella) mushrooms, sliced

1 onion, chopped

1 shallot, chopped

3 garlic cloves, minced

1 (18-ounce) tube prepared polenta, cut crosswise into 1-inch-thick slices

1 cup shredded mozzarella cheese

½ cup shredded Parmesan cheese

1. Preheat the oven to 450°F.

2. In a large oven-safe skillet, heat 1 tablespoon of olive oil and the butter over medium-high heat. Add the mushrooms, onion, shallot, and garlic and sauté for 5 to 7 minutes, until softened. Remove the vegetables with a slotted spoon and set aside in a medium bowl.

3. In the same skillet, heat the remaining 1 tablespoon of olive oil over medium-high heat. Working in batches if necessary, add the polenta slices in an even layer and cook for 4 to 5 minutes per side. When done, spread the mushroom mixture over the polenta slices. Sprinkle with the mozzarella and Parmesan, transfer the skillet to the oven, and bake for 5 minutes to melt the cheese.

4. Remove from the oven and serve.

**STORAGE:** Store leftovers in an airtight container in the refrigerator for up to 3 days.

**SERVING TIP:** This dish goes well with your favorite tomato sauce, if you want to change it up.

Per serving: Calories: 370; Total fat: 20g; Total carbs: 34g; Sugar: 3g; Protein: 14g; Fiber: 2g; Sodium: 612mg

Seafood Paella, *page 94*

# Fish and Seafood

# Seafood Paella

Serves: **4 or 5** | Prep time: **20 minutes** | Cook time: **35 minutes**

You can't do Spain any more justice than cooking its beloved paella. This may seem like an intimidating dish, but it's not, and we promise you'll love it. The mixture of rice, spice, and seafood works so wonderfully well, it's no surprise this recipe has been a regional favorite forever. Saffron and paprika add a lovely complex flavor and give the rice its trademark reddish tint. Paprika is made from finely grinding sweet red peppers and dried chile peppers. Paprika is not just delicious, but including this spice regularly in your diet can also help improve blood sugar, lower cholesterol, and support eye health.

1 tablespoon olive oil
8 ounces chicken
   andouille sausage
   links, sliced
1 small onion, diced
4 garlic cloves, minced
1 (12-ounce) can
   roasted red bell
   peppers, drained
   and chopped
1 (15-ounce) can
   diced tomatoes
2 cups uncooked
   Arborio rice

1 teaspoon paprika
½ teaspoon ground
   turmeric
Pinch saffron threads
Sea salt
Freshly ground
   black pepper
4 cups chicken broth
½ teaspoon red
   pepper flakes
1½ to 2 pounds
   mussels, scrubbed
   and debearded

1 pound littleneck
   clams, soaked for
   at least 20 minutes
   and scrubbed
1 pound large shrimp
   (31/35 count), peeled
   and deveined
½ cup frozen peas
¼ cup chopped fresh
   Italian parsley
Lemon wedges,
   for serving

1. In a large sauté pan, heat the olive oil over medium heat. Add the sausage and cook for 3 to 5 minutes. Add the onion, garlic, and roasted red peppers and sauté for about 5 minutes. Add the tomatoes and cook for 1 to 2 minutes to blend the ingredients.

2. Add the rice and sauté for 1 minute. Add the paprika, turmeric, and saffron and season with salt and black pepper. Sauté for 1 minute. Add the broth and red pepper flakes and increase the heat to medium-high to bring the mixture to a boil. Reduce the heat to low, cover, and simmer for 20 minutes, or until the liquid has been almost completely absorbed.

3. Add the mussels, clams, shrimp, and peas. Cover and increase the heat to medium. Cook for 7 to 10 minutes, until the seafood is just cooked through. (Discard any clams or mussels that do not open after 10 minutes of cooking.)

4. Garnish with the parsley and serve with lemon wedges alongside.

STORAGE: Store leftovers in an airtight container in the refrigerator for up to 3 days.

PREP TIP: Use a wide sauté pan to cook everything evenly, and try not to mix too much after adding the rice—the crispy rice at the bottom of the pan, known as the *soccarat*, is delicious.

Per serving: Calories: 706; Total fat: 15g; Total carbs: 98g; Sugar: 9g; Protein: 42g; Fiber: 7g; Sodium: 1,272mg

# Cod with Tomatoes and Garlic

Serves: **4** | Prep time: **10 minutes** | Cook time: **20 minutes** | **5-Ingredient** | **30-Minute**

Tomatoes are a constant in Mediterranean cooking, no matter the region, and combining cooked tomatoes with olive oil has several nutritional advantages. Cooked tomatoes contain an antioxidant called lycopene that becomes more bioavailable when the tomatoes are heated, while olive oil increases the absorption of fat-soluble vitamins and helps lower blood pressure. This light dish will keep you satisfied while delivering stellar health benefits from the fish and other ingredients.

1 pound cod or
  your favorite
  white-fleshed fish
Sea salt
Freshly ground
  black pepper

2 tablespoons olive oil
2 garlic cloves, minced
1 (15-ounce) can
  diced tomatoes, with
  their juices
¼ cup white wine

¼ cup chopped fresh
  Italian parsley

1. Pat the fish dry with paper towels and season with salt and pepper.

2. In a large skillet, heat the olive oil over medium heat. Add the cod and cook for 3 to 5 minutes on each side, or until cooked through. Transfer the fish to a plate, cover loosely with aluminum foil, and set aside.

3. Add the garlic to the skillet and sauté until fragrant, about 3 minutes. Add the tomatoes and wine and increase the heat to medium-high. Cook the tomato mixture for about 4 minutes. Season with salt and pepper.

4. Return the fish to the skillet and spoon the tomato mixture over it. Serve garnished with the parsley.

**STORAGE:** Store leftovers in an airtight container in the refrigerator for up to 3 days.

**SUBSTITUTION TIP:** Instead of canned tomatoes, use 1½ cups diced fresh tomatoes.

Per serving: Calories: 170; Total fat: 7g; Total carbs: 5g; Sugar: 3g; Protein: 18g; Fiber: 2g; Sodium: 507mg

# Baked Fish with Olives

Serves: **4** | Prep time: **10 minutes** | Cook time: **12 minutes** | **30-Minute**

The visual impact of this classic combination of ingredients will make eating this dish a pleasure. It tastes amazing, too. The acidity of the tomatoes balances nicely with the saltiness of the olives and the feta, and the fish absorbs these flavors wonderfully. The garlic contributes its usual kick, and shallots and onion add a unique flavor.

2 tablespoons olive oil
½ onion, chopped
2 shallots, diced
4 garlic cloves, minced
1 (28-ounce) can diced tomatoes, drained
Sea salt

Freshly ground black pepper
1 pound cod or other white-fleshed fish
½ cup chopped pitted kalamata olives

¼ cup crumbled feta cheese, for topping
¼ cup chopped fresh Italian parsley (optional)

1. Preheat the oven to 375°F.

2. In a large oven-safe skillet, heat the olive oil over medium-high heat. Add the onion, shallots, and garlic and sauté for 5 to 6 minutes, until softened. Add the tomatoes and season with salt and pepper. Cook, stirring occasionally, for 4 minutes.

3. Place the fish on top of the tomato mixture and evenly sprinkle with the olives and feta. Transfer the skillet to the oven and bake for 15 to 20 minutes, until the fish is cooked through.

4. Garnish with the parsley, if desired, and serve.

**STORAGE:** Store leftovers in an airtight container in the refrigerator for up to 2 days.

**SUBSTITUTION TIP:** This recipe works well with trout, tilapia, or mahi-mahi in place of the cod.

Per serving: Calories: 229; Total fat: 12g; Total carbs: 12g; Sugar: 6g; Protein: 21g; Fiber: 5g; Sodium: 724mg

# Pan-Seared Shrimp Skewers

Serves: **4** | Prep time: **20 minutes** | Cook time: **6 minutes** | **5-Ingredient** | **30-Minute**

Searching for a simple lemon shrimp recipe that goes perfectly over pasta or rice? Look no further than this speedy dish. You can also serve the tender pink shrimp skewers with baked potatoes or your favorite sautéed vegetables.

¼ cup olive oil

Zest and juice
  of 1 lemon

1 tablespoon
  dried oregano

¼ teaspoon red pepper
  flakes (optional)

Sea salt

Freshly ground
  black pepper

1 pound medium
  shrimp (36/40 count),
  peeled and deveined

1. In a large bowl, stir together the olive oil, lemon zest, oregano, and red pepper flakes, if desired. Season with salt and black pepper. Add the shrimp and mix well. Cover the bowl with plastic wrap and refrigerate for 15 minutes.

2. Remove the bowl from the refrigerator and thread the shrimp onto skewers. Discard any remaining marinade.

3. Heat a large skillet over medium heat. Place the skewers in the skillet and sear the shrimp for 3 to 4 minutes per side, until just cooked through.

4. Drizzle with the lemon juice and serve.

**STORAGE:** Store leftovers in an airtight container in the refrigerator for up to 2 days.

**SERVING TIP:** Top a lovely pilaf or couscous dish with a couple of these skewers for a light meal.

Per serving: Calories: 204; Total fat: 15g; Total carbs: 2g; Sugar: 0g; Protein: 15g; Fiber: 0g; Sodium: 581mg

# Mediterranean Shrimp Stir-Fry

Serves: **4** | Prep time: **10 minutes** | Cook time: **10 minutes** | **30-Minute**

Shrimp, zucchini, asparagus, herbs, and feta make a winning combination for a light, healthy dish. Add a full-bodied white wine to round out the meal.

¼ cup freshly squeezed lemon juice

¼ cup olive oil

½ teaspoon onion powder

½ teaspoon garlic powder

14 ounces medium shrimp (36/40 count), peeled and deveined

½ onion, chopped

2 zucchini, quartered lengthwise and sliced into ½-inch pieces

½ bunch asparagus, woody ends trimmed, chopped

1 tomato, chopped

1 garlic clove, minced

1½ teaspoons dried basil

½ teaspoon dried oregano

¼ teaspoon sea salt

¼ teaspoon freshly ground black pepper

Dash red pepper flakes

½ cup kalamata olives, pitted

¼ cup crumbled feta cheese, for topping

1. In a small bowl, stir together the lemon juice, olive oil, onion powder, and garlic powder. Add the shrimp, mix well, and cover with plastic wrap. Marinate in the refrigerator for 10 minutes.

2. Heat a large skillet over medium-high heat. Add the marinated shrimp (discard the marinade) and cook until pink, 3 to 5 minutes. Remove the shrimp with a slotted spoon and set aside in a medium bowl.

3. In the same skillet, sauté the onion over medium-high heat for 3 minutes. Add the zucchini, asparagus, tomato, garlic, basil, oregano, salt, black pepper, and red pepper flakes and cook for 2 to 3 minutes.

4. Return the shrimp to the skillet, add the olives, and stir to combine.

5. Serve topped with the feta.

**STORAGE:** Store leftovers in an airtight container in the refrigerator for up to 2 days.

**SUBSTITUTION TIP:** You can use larger or smaller shrimp in this recipe as long as you adjust the cooking time accordingly.

---

Per serving: Calories: 276; Total fat: 19g; Total carbs: 11g; Sugar: 5g; Protein: 18g; Fiber: 3g; Sodium: 721mg

# Cod with Spinach-Artichoke Spread

Serves: **4** | Prep time: **10 minutes** | Cook time: **15 minutes** | **30-Minute**

Topping a piece of cod with your delicious spinach-artichoke dip: Is this crazy? Yes. Is it delicious? You bet! Water-packed artichoke hearts work best here because the oil from the marinated variety can change the texture of the dip. If you have any leftover dip, serve it with pita bread or cut-up vegetables as a healthy snack.

4 tablespoons olive oil, divided

4 (5-ounce) fresh or thawed frozen cod fillets

1 jalapeño pepper, seeded and chopped

1 (15-ounce) can water-packed artichoke hearts, drained and chopped

1 (10-ounce) bag frozen spinach, thawed and drained

2 cups plain full-fat Greek yogurt

1½ cups grated Parmesan cheese

1 (8-ounce) package cream cheese

2 tablespoons unsalted butter

3 garlic cloves, minced

7 kalamata olives, pitted and chopped

1. In a large skillet, heat 2 tablespoons of olive oil over medium heat. Add the cod and cook for 4 to 5 minutes on each side, until white and opaque throughout. Transfer the fish to a plate, cover loosely with aluminum foil to keep it warm, and set aside.

2. In the same skillet, heat the remaining 2 tablespoons of olive oil over medium-high heat. Add the jalapeño and sauté for 3 to 4 minutes, until fragrant. Add the artichoke hearts, spinach, yogurt, Parmesan, cream cheese, butter, garlic, and olives and cook, stirring frequently, until the cheese has melted, 3 to 4 minutes. Simmer for 3 minutes more, then remove from the heat.

3. Place a cod fillet on each of four plates and spoon the artichoke mixture evenly over each piece of fish. Serve.

**STORAGE:** Store any leftover fish and dip in separate airtight containers in the refrigerator for up to 3 days. Reheat separately before serving.

Per serving: Calories: 789; Total fat: 55g; Total carbs: 28g; Sugar: 9g; Protein: 48g; Fiber: 10g; Sodium: 1,040mg

# Shrimp Saganaki

Serves: **4** | Prep time: **15 minutes** | Cook time: **15 minutes** | **30-Minute**

We love this tasty, super easy dish so much. This recipe is also pretty versatile. Jane's brother and his wife pour it over pasta.

1 pound medium shrimp (36/40 count), peeled and deveined
½ cup plus 1 tablespoon olive oil, divided
½ cup white wine

Zest of 1 lemon
2 garlic cloves, minced
Sea salt
Freshly ground black pepper
½ cup chopped onion

1 tomato, diced
½ cup crumbled feta cheese
¼ cup chopped fresh Italian parsley

1. Preheat the oven to 400°F.

2. In a large bowl, stir together the shrimp, ½ cup of olive oil, the wine, lemon zest, and garlic. Season with salt and pepper and set aside.

3. In a Dutch oven, heat the remaining 1 tablespoon of olive oil over medium heat. Add the onion and sauté for 5 minutes, or until softened. Add the tomato and the shrimp mixture and cook for 3 minutes.

4. Transfer the Dutch oven to the oven and bake for 7 minutes, or until the shrimp are just cooked through. Remove from the oven, top with the feta, and bake for 1 to 2 minutes more.

5. Garnish with the parsley and serve.

**STORAGE:** Store leftovers in an airtight container in the refrigerator for up to 3 days.

**WINE PAIRING TIP:** Get a decent dry white wine to use for the saganaki, and enjoy the rest of the bottle with dinner.

Per serving: Calories: 321; Total fat: 22g; Total carbs: 6g; Sugar: 3g; Protein: 19g; Fiber: 1g; Sodium: 759mg

# Cod and Potatoes in Avgolemono

Serves: **4** | Prep time: **10 minutes** | Cook time: **25 minutes**

If you've never had avgolemono, you're in for a treat. The tangy lemony broth pairs perfectly with the fish to create a flavor profile like no other. The potato "side" for this meal is cooked right along with the fish, soaking up all the delightful avgolemono. Buttery fingerling potatoes are lovely as well.

4 cups chicken broth

1 pound baby red
   potatoes, quartered

¼ cup chopped onion

3 garlic cloves, minced

Sea salt

Freshly ground
   black pepper

4 (5-ounce) cod fillets

2 large eggs

Juice of 1 lemon

1. In a large stockpot, bring the broth to a boil over high heat. Add the potatoes, onion, and garlic. Season with salt and pepper, cover, reduce the heat to low, and simmer for 15 minutes. Add the cod and simmer for 7 to 10 minutes more, until the fish is cooked through.

2. While the cod is simmering, in a small bowl, whisk together the eggs and lemon juice. While whisking continuously, slowly add 1 cup of the hot broth to the bowl with the egg mixture and whisk for a few seconds more to temper the egg mixture. Pour the mixture from the bowl back into the stockpot and stir to combine. Serve.

**STORAGE:** Store leftovers in an airtight container in the refrigerator for up to 3 days.

**COOKING TIP:** Make sure to temper the eggs, because adding them directly to the pot with the hot broth will cause them to curdle.

Per serving: Calories: 241; Total fat: 4g; Total carbs: 21g; Sugar: 2g; Protein: 30g; Fiber: 2g; Sodium: 172mg

# Tomato and White Beans with Garlic Shrimp

Serves: **4** | Prep time: **10 minutes** | Cook time: **10 minutes** | **5-Ingredient** | **30-Minute**

A quick skillet dinner is just the ticket for evenings when you are running late or just don't have the energy to make a more elaborate spread. Mixing tomatoes, white beans, and shrimp with a nice punch of garlic is always delicious. Add a sprinkle of salty feta as a tasty topping to lift this dish to another culinary level.

3 tablespoons olive oil
½ onion, diced
4 garlic cloves, minced
1 (15-ounce) can diced tomatoes, with their juices

2 (15-ounce) cans white beans, drained and rinsed
½ to ¾ cup water

1 pound medium shrimp (36/40 count), peeled and deveined
¼ cup chopped fresh Italian parsley

1. In a large skillet, heat the olive oil over medium-high heat. Add the onion and garlic and sauté for 4 minutes. Add the tomatoes and cook for 2 minutes. Add the beans and water and bring to a simmer.

2. Add the shrimp and simmer for 3 to 4 minutes, until the shrimp are just cooked through.

3. Serve garnished with the parsley.

**STORAGE:** Store leftovers in an airtight container in the refrigerator for up to 3 days.

**INGREDIENT TIP:** Feel free to add some red pepper flakes, if you like—a little heat works beautifully in this dish and complements the acidity from the tomatoes.

Per serving: Calories: 385; Total fat: 12g; Total carbs: 41g; Sugar: 4g; Protein: 30g; Fiber: 11g; Sodium: 676mg

# White Wine–Steamed Mussels with Spanish Chorizo

Serves: **4** | Prep time: **10 minutes** | Cook time: **15 minutes** | **30-Minute**

Mussels in white wine are divine. The hint of spiciness from the chorizo balances the spices and garlic without overpowering the fresh mollusks. If you've never cooked mussels before, this recipe is a great introduction.

1 tablespoon olive oil

8 ounces cured (Spanish) chorizo, sliced

1 onion, chopped

3 garlic cloves, diced

1 teaspoon ground cumin

1 teaspoon sea salt

1 tomato, chopped

2 tablespoons unsalted butter

½ cup white wine

1 pound mussels, scrubbed and debearded

½ cup coarsely chopped fresh cilantro, for garnish

1 lemon, cut into wedges, for serving

1.  In a Dutch oven, heat the olive oil over medium heat. Add the chorizo and cook for about 2 minutes. Add the onion, garlic, cumin, and salt and sauté for 5 minutes, or until the vegetables are softened. Add the tomato and cook for 3 minutes. Add the butter and cook until it has melted, about 1 minute.

2.  Add the wine and increase the heat to medium-high. Add the mussels and cook for 5 to 8 minutes, until the mussels have opened. Discard any unopened mussels.

3.  Evenly divide the mussels, chorizo, and broth among four bowls. Garnish with the cilantro and serve with the lemon wedges alongside.

**SERVING TIP:** This dish is also delicious served over pasta.

**VARIATION TIP:** You can substitute Italian sausage for the chorizo, if that's all you have on hand or chorizo is unavailable.

Per serving: Calories: 410; Total fat: 32g; Total carbs: 8g; Sugar: 2g; Protein: 18g; Fiber: 1g; Sodium: 924mg

# Foil-Baked Fish

Serves: **4** | Prep time: **10 minutes** | Cook time: **20 minutes** | **5-Ingredient** | **30-Minute**

This cooking method is called *al cartoccio* in Italian and *en papillote* in French, and the idea is to enclose the ingredients completely to keep all the juices and seasonings sealed inside the packet. Cod baked in foil packets is one of the easiest fish recipes in this book. You can get a little creative by using different herbs and spices—we like the classic garlic and lemon, but you can add whatever you like best.

4 (5-ounce) cod or other white-fleshed fish fillets

2 to 3 tablespoons olive oil

2 to 3 garlic cloves, minced

1 tablespoon freshly squeezed lemon juice

Sea salt

Freshly ground black pepper

1. Preheat the oven to 400°F. Cut four 12-inch squares of aluminum foil and lay them on a clean work surface.

2. Pat the fish dry with paper towels and place one fillet on each sheet of foil.

3. In a small bowl, mix the olive oil, garlic, and lemon juice and season with salt and pepper. Brush the oil mixture over both sides of the fish. Fold the foil over the fish to enclose it and crimp the edges of the foil to seal.

4. Place the foil packets on a baking sheet and bake for 15 to 20 minutes, until the fish is cooked through and flakes easily with a fork.

5. Remove from the oven and serve. Be sure to tell your guests to be careful of the hot steam when opening their packets.

**STORAGE:** Store leftovers in an airtight container in the refrigerator for up to 3 days.

**VARIATION TIP:** Try adding some red pepper flakes, lemon pepper, jerk seasoning, or herbs as well as a little sliver of butter to each packet to vary the flavors.

Per serving: Calories: 179; Total fat: 8g; Total carbs: 1g; Sugar: 1g; Protein: 25g; Fiber: 1g; Sodium: 116mg

# Fish Tacos

Serves: **4** | Prep time: **15 minutes** | Cook time: **20 minutes**

Fish tacos are a staple in our home. Our go-to recipe is this one, which mixes creamy Greek yogurt with lime juice to create a thick, healthy sauce that brings the entire dish together. A couple of slices of avocado or ripe mango would be spectacular, if you have them.

1 pound cod, cut into
  1-inch chunks
Zest and juice of 1 lime
2 tablespoons olive
  oil, divided
¼ teaspoon chili powder

¼ teaspoon
  ground cumin
Sea salt
Freshly ground
  black pepper
2 cups chopped cabbage

¼ cup chopped
  fresh cilantro
½ cup plain full-fat
  Greek yogurt
8 (6-inch) corn or
  flour tortillas

1. In a large bowl, stir together the cod, half the lime juice, 1 tablespoon of olive oil, the chili powder, and the cumin. Season with salt and pepper and set aside.

2. In a medium bowl, combine the remaining lime juice, the cabbage, and the cilantro and set aside.

3. In a medium bowl, stir together the yogurt and lime zest, season with salt and pepper, and set aside.

4. Heat a large skillet over medium-high heat. Working in batches, warm the tortillas for 2 minutes per side. Wrap in a clean kitchen cloth or place in a tortilla warmer to keep them warm; set aside.

5. In the same skillet, heat the remaining 1 tablespoon of olive oil over medium-high heat. Add the cod and cook for 4 to 6 minutes (depending on thickness), until cooked through.

6. Divide the fish evenly among the tortillas and top each with the cabbage mixture and yogurt sauce. Serve.

**STORAGE:** Store the fish, yogurt sauce, and cabbage mixture in separate airtight containers in the refrigerator for up to 3 days. Reheat the cod and assemble the tacos just before serving.

**SUBSTITUTION TIP:** Salmon works nicely in this recipe because it is a firm-fleshed fish, and its strong flavor is not overpowered by the other ingredients.

Per serving: Calories: 290; Total fat: 10g; Total carbs: 30g; Sugar: 4g; Protein: 22g; Fiber: 4g; Sodium: 420mg

Chicken Skewers | Souvlakis, *page 111*

# Chicken

# Bomba Chicken with Chickpeas

Serves: **4** | Prep time: **10 minutes** | Cook time: **30 minutes**

We love spicing up our dinners with bomba, a delicious hot pepper sauce from Italy. Bomba goes with anything, but we think it pairs exceptionally well with juicy chicken thighs. Add some beans and vegetables to the dish, and you have yourself a fantastic and quick meal.

2 pounds boneless, skinless chicken thighs
Sea salt
Freshly ground black pepper

2 tablespoons olive oil, divided
1 onion, chopped
3 garlic cloves, minced
1 cup chicken broth
1 tablespoon bomba sauce or harissa

2 (15-ounce) cans chickpeas, drained and rinsed
¼ cup chopped fresh Italian parsley

1.  Season the chicken thighs generously with salt and pepper.

2.  In a large skillet, heat 1 tablespoon of olive oil over medium-high heat. Add the chicken and cook until browned, 2 to 3 minutes per side. Transfer the chicken to a plate and set aside.

3.  In the same skillet, heat the remaining 1 tablespoon of olive oil. Add the onion and garlic and sauté for 4 to 5 minutes, until softened. Return the chicken to the skillet, then add the broth and bomba sauce. Bring to a boil, reduce the heat to low, cover, and simmer for 15 minutes, or until the chicken is cooked through.

4.  Add the chickpeas and simmer for 5 minutes more.

5.  Garnish with the parsley and serve.

**STORAGE:** Store leftovers in an airtight container in the refrigerator for up to 3 days.

**SUBSTITUTION TIP:** You can find bomba sauce at Trader Joe's and at some online retailers. If you can't find it and don't have harissa on hand as a substitute, spice up this recipe using ¼ to ½ teaspoon red pepper flakes or ¼ teaspoon cayenne pepper instead.

Per serving: Calories: 552; Total fat: 19g; Total carbs: 37g; Sugar: 7g; Protein: 56g; Fiber: 10g; Sodium: 267mg

# Chicken Skewers | Souvlakis

Serves: **4** | Prep time: **10 minutes**, plus marinating time | Cook time: **7 minutes**

Greek souvlakis are delicious meat skewers with a simple herb marinade. They are delicious and straightforward to make. The flavor profile in this marinade is perfectly balanced, but you can always adjust the seasonings to your liking (just remember to taste it before adding the raw poultry). Serve these skewers with a pilaf, or tuck the meat into a pita with some shredded lettuce and a dollop of sour cream.

¼ cup olive oil

Zest of 1 lemon

Juice of 2 lemons

2 tablespoons dried oregano

1 tablespoon dried thyme

2 garlic cloves, minced

Sea salt

Freshly ground black pepper

3 pounds boneless, skinless chicken breasts, cut into 2-inch cubes

1. In a large bowl, stir together the olive oil, lemon zest, lemon juice, oregano, thyme, and garlic. Season with salt and pepper and mix well. Add the chicken and stir to coat thoroughly. Cover the bowl and refrigerate for at least 20 to 30 minutes.

2. Remove the chicken from the refrigerator and thread the chicken pieces onto skewers, using 4 or 5 pieces per skewer.

3. Heat a cast-iron skillet over medium-high heat. Working in batches, place the skewers in the skillet, about 3 per batch, and cook, turning frequently, for 5 to 7 minutes, until the chicken is cooked through and has an internal temperature of 165°F. Repeat with the remaining skewers. Serve.

**STORAGE:** Store leftovers in an airtight container in the refrigerator for up to 3 days.

**VARIATION TIP:** If you're using wooden skewers, soak them in water while you're marinating the chicken to prevent them from scorching. You can alternate threading the marinated chicken with chunks of fresh vegetables. These skewers are also lovely grilled.

Per serving: Calories: 504; Total fat: 19g; Total carbs: 4g; Sugar: 1g; Protein: 76g; Fiber: 1g; Sodium: 214mg

# Chicken Tagine

Serves: **4** | Prep time: **15 minutes** | Cook time: **35 minutes**

Tagines are a staple in Moroccan culture. Traditional recipes tend to call for hours of simmering, but our version has a much shorter cook time. The simple veggie-and-chicken combination takes on a little heat from the harissa and subtle sweetness from the dried apricots.

3 tablespoons olive oil

1 onion, sliced

2 carrots, cut into long ribbons

2 red bell peppers, coarsely chopped

3 garlic cloves, minced

3 pounds boneless, skinless chicken thighs

1 cup chicken broth

1 tablespoon tomato paste

1 teaspoon ground coriander

½ teaspoon ground turmeric

1 to 2 tablespoons harissa

¼ cup chopped dried apricots

Sea salt

Freshly ground black pepper

1. In a large stockpot, heat the olive oil over medium-high heat. Add the onion, carrots, bell peppers, and garlic and sauté for 5 to 7 minutes, until softened. Add the chicken and cook, turning to brown the chicken evenly on all sides, for about 7 minutes.

2. In a small bowl, stir together the broth, tomato paste, coriander, turmeric, and harissa until well combined. Add the broth mixture to the stockpot and stir well. Add the apricots and season with salt and pepper.

3. Bring to a boil, reduce the heat to low, cover, and simmer for 20 minutes, or until the chicken is cooked through and has an internal temperature of 165°F. Serve.

**STORAGE:** Store leftovers in an airtight container in the refrigerator for up to 3 days.

**VARIATION TIP:** Feel free to use any vegetables you have on hand.

Per serving: Calories: 570; Total fat: 25g; Total carbs: 16g; Sugar: 10g; Protein: 69g; Fiber: 4g; Sodium: 390mg

# Sausage, Chicken, and Beans

Serves: **4** | Prep time: **10 minutes** | Cook time: **30 minutes**

In the South of France, there is a classic dish called cassoulet, which simmers for hours and is utterly delicious. Cassoulet is just a posh way of saying "white bean stew," but it got its French name because traditionally, a cassoulet was cooked in a special earthenware pot called a *cassolo*. In this speedy version, you will be using a skillet, and the cooking time is much shorter. Feel free to mix it up with your favorite meats instead of chicken, or make the dish vegetarian.

2 tablespoons olive oil
1 onion, diced
2 carrots, chopped
2 celery stalks, chopped
4 garlic cloves, minced
1 shallot, diced
1 pound boneless, skinless chicken thighs

1 pound pork sausages, casings removed, cut into 2-inch pieces
2 tomatoes, diced, or 1 (15-ounce) can diced tomatoes with their juices
1 tablespoon tomato paste
½ teaspoon dried thyme

2 bay leaves
Sea salt
Freshly ground black pepper
½ cup chicken broth, as needed
2 (15-ounce) cans cannellini beans, drained and rinsed

1. In a large skillet, heat the olive oil over medium-high heat. Add the onion, carrots, celery, garlic, and shallot and sauté for 5 minutes, or until the vegetables are softened. Add the chicken and sausage and sauté, turning to brown the chicken on all sides, for 5 minutes. Add the diced tomatoes, tomato paste, thyme, and bay leaves. Season with salt and pepper and add half the broth.

2. Bring to a boil, reduce the heat to medium-low, and simmer for 15 minutes, or until the chicken is cooked through. Add the beans and cook for 5 minutes, adding more broth as needed so that the mixture is just slightly soupy. Serve.

**STORAGE:** Store leftovers in an airtight container in the refrigerator for up to 3 days.

**COOKING TIP:** You want about 1½ inches of liquid in the pan, so you may need to add a little more broth (or a little less, especially if you're using canned tomatoes).

Per serving: Calories: 804; Total fat: 48g; Total carbs: 41g; Sugar: 5g; Protein: 52g; Fiber: 11g; Sodium: 912mg

# Chicken Gyro

Serves: **4** | Prep time: **20 minutes** | Cook time: **10 minutes**

This is a lighter gyro, made with chicken in place of the classic beef-and-lamb combination you'll find in traditional versions sold at your local Greek festival. The trick here is using good tzatziki and tempting warm pitas. The gyros are so delicious mainly because the flavors of the ingredients blend together harmoniously.

3 tablespoons olive oil

Zest and juice of
  ½ lemon

1 tablespoon
  dried oregano

1½ teaspoons
  dried thyme

1 garlic clove, minced

¼ teaspoon sea salt

¼ teaspoon freshly
  ground black pepper

2 pounds boneless,
  skinless chicken
  thighs, cut into
  ½-inch-thick strips

4 pita breads

3 Roma (plum)
  tomatoes, diced

½ red onion,
  thinly sliced

½ cup Tzatziki
  (page 35)

¼ cup crumbled
  feta cheese

1. In a large bowl, stir together the olive oil, lemon zest, lemon juice, oregano, thyme, garlic, salt, and pepper. Add the chicken and toss to evenly coat. Cover the bowl and marinate in the refrigerator for 30 minutes.

2. Heat a large skillet over medium-high heat. Add the chicken (discard the marinade) and cook for 7 to 10 minutes, until cooked through. Transfer the chicken to a plate.

3. Place the pitas on a clean work surface and top each with 3 or 4 strips of chicken. Evenly divide the tomatoes, onion, tzatziki, and feta among the pitas.

4. Fold the pitas over to enclose the toppings and serve.

**STORAGE:** Store any leftover cooked chicken in an airtight container in the refrigerator for up to 3 days. Assemble the gyros just before serving.

**SERVING TIP:** The chicken can be served with a cold salad like Tabbouleh (page 40) or alongside a rice or couscous dish instead of stuffed into pitas.

Per serving: Calories: 506; Total fat: 23g; Total carbs: 23g; Sugar: 5g; Protein: 50g; Fiber: 4g; Sodium: 523mg

# Chicken Avgolemono

Serves: **4** | Prep time: **10 minutes** | Cook time: **50 minutes** | **5-Ingredient**

Growing up, this was Kenton's "chicken noodle soup." There isn't a Greek anywhere who's ever turned down Yiayia's (Grandma's) avgolemono. This egg-lemon soup is heavenly. Sometimes it is put together with just rice or orzo, but we've always made it with chicken.

1½ pounds boneless, skinless chicken breasts

6 cups chicken broth, as needed

¾ cup dried Greek orzo

3 large eggs

Juice of 2 lemons

Sea salt

Freshly ground black pepper

1. Place the chicken in a stockpot and add enough broth to cover the chicken by 1 inch. Bring to a boil over high heat, then reduce the heat to low, cover, and simmer for 30 to 45 minutes, until the chicken is cooked through. Remove the chicken from the stockpot and set aside in a medium bowl.

2. Increase the heat to medium-high and bring the broth back to a boil. Add the orzo and cook for 7 to 10 minutes, until tender.

3. While the orzo is cooking, shred the chicken with two forks and return it to the pot when orzo is done.

4. Crack the eggs into a small bowl and whisk until frothy, then whisk in the lemon juice. While whisking continuously, slowly pour in 1 cup of the hot broth to temper the eggs. Pour the egg mixture back into the pot and stir. Simmer for 1 minute more, season with salt and pepper, and serve.

**STORAGE:** Store leftovers in an airtight container in the refrigerator for up to 3 days.

**VARIATION TIP:** The egg-lemon broth makes a beautiful base for many different soups. Try adding fish or veggies instead of chicken for a different but equally delicious version.

Per serving: Calories: 391; Total fat: 9g; Total carbs: 29g; Sugar: 1g; Protein: 46g; Fiber: 1g; Sodium: 171mg

# Chicken Pasta Salad with Spinach

Serves: **4** | Prep time: **15 minutes** | Cook time: **45 minutes**

In our household, we like to experiment with all kinds of pasta salads, because pasta is tasty and inexpensive, and it combines well with many different ingredients. This recipe has a nice balance of vegetables and poultry and tastes incredibly fresh, especially after chilling in the refrigerator. Feel free to alter the herbs and switch up the ingredients to create your own unique variation.

1 pound boneless, skinless chicken thighs or breasts

1½ cups dried farfalle (bow-tie) pasta

½ (15-ounce) can chickpeas, drained and rinsed

2 cups fresh baby spinach

½ English cucumber, chopped

¼ cup sun-dried tomatoes, chopped

¼ cup shredded Parmesan cheese

¼ cup shredded carrot

Juice of ½ lemon

2 tablespoons olive oil

½ teaspoon dried thyme

¼ teaspoon dried marjoram

Sea salt

Freshly ground black pepper

1. Put the chicken in a large stockpot and add enough water to cover the chicken by 1 inch. Bring the water to a boil over high heat, then reduce the heat to low, and simmer for 30 minutes, or until the chicken is cooked through. Remove the chicken from the pot and set it aside on a plate.

2. Bring the water back to a boil over high heat. Add the pasta and cook according to the package directions until al dente, 10 to 12 minutes. Drain the pasta and rinse with cold water to stop the cooking process. Transfer the pasta to a large bowl.

3. Chop the chicken into 2-inch pieces and add them to the bowl with the pasta. Add the chickpeas, spinach, cucumber, sun-dried tomatoes, Parmesan, carrot, lemon juice, olive oil, thyme, and marjoram and toss to mix well.

4. Season with salt and pepper and serve.

**STORAGE:** Store leftovers in an airtight container in the refrigerator for up to 3 days.

**VARIATION TIP:** Top with feta cheese for a nice salty bite. If you have leftover cooked chicken from another meal, you can use it in this dish—just skip step 1 of the recipe.

---

Per serving: Calories: 439; Total fat: 15g; Total carbs: 43g; Sugar: 5g; Protein: 33g; Fiber: 5g; Sodium: 289mg

# Chicken with White Wine

Serves: **4** | Prep time: **5 minutes** | Cook time: **45 minutes**

This simple chicken dish is an ideal justification for opening a bottle of wine after a long week (if you need a reason). The pairing of garlic, rosemary, and mushrooms elevates the chicken breasts to a restaurant-quality level. The recipe is easy to prepare, healthy, and delicious. An added bonus? You only need ¼ cup of the wine, so the rest of the bottle is there for you to sip while waiting for dinner—what more could you ask for?

1 tablespoon olive oil
2 pounds boneless,
  skinless chicken
  breasts

8 ounces cremini
  (baby bella)
  mushrooms, quartered
½ onion, diced
3 garlic cloves, minced
¼ cup white wine

¼ teaspoon chopped
  fresh rosemary
Sea salt
Freshly ground
  black pepper

1. In a large skillet, heat the olive oil over medium-high heat. Add the chicken and brown, turning once, 5 to 7 minutes. Transfer the chicken to a plate and set aside.

2. Add the mushrooms, onion, and garlic to the skillet and cook for 7 to 10 minutes, until the vegetables are softened.

3. Return the chicken to the skillet and add the wine and rosemary. Season with salt and pepper and bring to a boil. Reduce the heat to low, cover, and simmer for 20 to 30 minutes, until the chicken is cooked through. Serve.

**STORAGE:** Store leftovers in an airtight container in the refrigerator for up to 3 days.

**COOKING TIP:** You can substitute chicken broth for the wine if you don't have any on hand or prefer to avoid using alcohol.

Per serving: Calories: 453; Total fat: 25g; Total carbs: 5g; Sugar: 2g; Protein: 49g; Fiber: 1g; Sodium: 188mg

# Chicken in Cream Sauce

Serves: **6** | Prep time: **10 minutes** | Cook time: **35 minutes**

The cream sauce is rich enough to carry all the herbs in this dish and coats the chicken beautifully. Tomatoes on the vine have a sweetness and depth of flavor not found in the conventionally grown artificially ripened varieties. These deep red tomatoes are picked before they are completely ripe and allowed to mature naturally, so all the flavor is concentrated.

3 tablespoons olive oil

6 (4-ounce) boneless, skinless chicken breasts

½ zucchini, chopped into 2-inch pieces

1 celery stalk, chopped

1 red bell pepper, thinly sliced

2 tomatoes on the vine, chopped

3 garlic cloves, minced

½ teaspoon dried thyme

½ teaspoon dried marjoram

½ teaspoon dried basil

½ cup baby spinach

1 cup heavy (whipping) cream

¼ cup chopped fresh Italian parsley (optional)

1. In a large skillet, heat the olive oil over medium-high heat. Add the chicken and cook for 8 to 10 minutes on each side, until cooked through. Transfer the chicken to a plate and set aside.

2. Add the zucchini, celery, bell pepper, tomatoes, and garlic and sauté for 8 to 10 minutes, until the vegetables are softened. Add the thyme, marjoram, and basil and cook for 1 minute. Add the spinach and cook until wilted, about 3 minutes.

3. Add the cream and mix well. Return the chicken to the skillet and cook until warmed through, about 4 minutes.

4. Garnish with the parsley, if desired, and serve.

**STORAGE:** Store leftovers in an airtight container in the refrigerator for up to 3 days.

**COOKING TIP:** If you plan to freeze some portion of this dish, omit the cream before freezing, then add it when you are reheating.

Per serving: Calories: 341; Total fat: 24g; Total carbs: 5g; Sugar: 4g; Protein: 27g; Fiber: 1g; Sodium: 83mg

# Garlic and Oregano Roasted Chicken

Serves: **4 to 6** | Prep time: **10 minutes** | Cook time: **1 hour 40 minutes** | **5-Ingredient**

There's something comforting about roasting a whole chicken—it's a culinary achievement that will make you feel like a professional chef. The enticing scent of the bird will fill your home as it cooks, and this simple preparation will delight everyone. Feel free to get creative with spices and herbs to produce a family-favorite meal.

1 (3½- to 4-pound) whole chicken

Zest and juice of 1 lemon

4 tablespoons dried oregano, divided

3 garlic cloves, crushed

3 tablespoons olive oil

2 tablespoons unsalted butter, at room temperature

Sea salt

Freshly ground black pepper

1. Preheat the oven to 375°F.

2. Place the chicken in a roasting pan.

3. In a small bowl, stir together the lemon zest, half the lemon juice, 3 tablespoons of oregano, and the garlic and place the mixture in the chicken's cavity. Place the two juiced lemon halves in the cavity as well.

4. Rub the olive oil, butter, and remaining lemon juice over the chicken. Sprinkle with the remaining 1 tablespoon of oregano and season with salt and pepper.

5. Roast the chicken, basting it occasionally with the pan juices, for 20 minutes per pound, plus an additional 20 minutes, until the skin is golden brown and the juices run clear when the thigh is pierced. When there are 15 minutes left in the cooking time, cover the chicken loosely with aluminum foil to prevent the skin from burning.

6. Carve the chicken and spoon the juices from the bottom of the pan onto each plate. Serve.

**STORAGE:** Store any leftover chicken in an airtight container in the refrigerator for up to 3 days.

**COOKING TIP:** Your cooking time will change based on the weight of the chicken. Adjust accordingly and use a meat thermometer to accurately gauge doneness (chicken should be cooked to 165°F; measure the temperature at the thickest part of a thigh, without touching bone). Feel free to throw some vegetables into the pan with the chicken to serve as a side dish.

Per serving: Calories: 670; Total fat: 52g; Total carbs: 3g; Sugar: 0g; Protein: 45g; Fiber: 1g; Sodium: 361mg

# Chicken with Lemon and Olives

Serves: **4 or 5** | Prep time: **15 minutes** | Cook time: **45 minutes**

Inspired by a dish served on the Greek island of Corfu, this recipe combines unusual flavors that work amazingly well together. For even more of a lemony boost, add ½ teaspoon lemon zest along with the spinach at the end.

2 tablespoons olive oil
⅓ cup all-purpose flour
¼ teaspoon paprika
½ teaspoon dried basil
⅛ teaspoon red
  pepper flakes
Sea salt

Freshly ground
  black pepper
3 pounds chicken thighs
1 cup halved pitted
  kalamata olives
2 carrots, diced
1 onion, diced

3 garlic cloves, minced
½ cup water
Juice of ½ lemon
1 cup fresh
  baby spinach

1. In a large skillet, heat the olive oil over medium heat.

2. In a small bowl, mix together the flour, paprika, basil, and red pepper flakes. Season with salt and black pepper.

3. Dredge the chicken in the flour mixture, shake off any excess, and place in the skillet. Cook the chicken, turning occasionally, for 6 to 8 minutes, until browned. Transfer the chicken to a plate and set aside.

4. Add the olives, carrots, onion, and garlic to the skillet and sauté for 3 to 5 minutes. Add the water to the skillet and bring to a boil. Return the chicken to the skillet, reduce the heat to low, cover, and simmer for 25 to 30 minutes, until the chicken is cooked through. Add the lemon juice when there are 5 minutes left in the cooking time.

5. Add the spinach, cover, and remove from the heat. Keep covered for a few minutes until the spinach has wilted, then serve.

STORAGE: Store leftovers in an airtight container in the refrigerator for up to 3 days.

COOKING TIP: You can use chicken legs or breasts instead of thighs, but adjust the cooking time and use a meat thermometer to check for doneness (chicken should be cooked to 165°F).

Per serving: Calories: 578; Total fat: 24g; Total carbs: 17g; Sugar: 3g; Protein: 69g; Fiber: 3g; Sodium: 638mg

# Chicken with Mushroom Sauce

Serves: **4** | Prep time: **10 minutes** | Cook time: **40 minutes**

When we traveled to Paris, we stayed in Saint-Germain-des-Prés, where we found a small restaurant that cooked a delectable version of this dish. It was so inspiring, we immediately re-created the recipe when we got home, and have cooked it often since then. The garlic-mushroom cream sauce is an exceptional blending of textures and flavors. Sometimes we make this dish without the chicken and spoon the sauce over toast, vegetables, or meats.

2 tablespoons olive oil, divided
2 pounds boneless, skinless chicken thighs
1 small onion, diced

2 garlic cloves, minced
3 tablespoons unsalted butter
8 ounces cremini (baby bella) mushrooms, chopped

½ cup pinot grigio
½ cup chicken broth
1 cup heavy (whipping) cream

1.  In a sauté pan, heat 1 tablespoon of olive oil over medium-high heat. Add the chicken and cook, turning it occasionally, for 12 to 15 minutes, until cooked through. Transfer the chicken to a plate and set aside.

2.  In the same sauté pan, heat the remaining 1 tablespoon of olive oil over medium-high heat. Add the onion and garlic and sauté until the onion is translucent, 5 to 7 minutes. Add the butter and mushrooms and cook for 5 to 7 minutes, until the mushrooms have released their liquid.

3.  Add the wine and use a spoon to scrape up any browned bits from the bottom of the pan. Simmer for 3 to 4 minutes. Add the broth and simmer until it has reduced by about three-quarters, about 5 minutes. Add the cream and simmer for 3 to 5 minutes. Return the chicken to the pan and cook until heated through, about 4 minutes.

4.  Serve.

**STORAGE:** Store leftovers in an airtight container in the refrigerator for up to 3 days.

**COOKING TIP:** You can add cornstarch to the sauce to thicken it more quickly.

Per serving: Calories: 662; Total fat: 47g; Total carbs: 7g; Sugar: 4g; Protein: 47g; Fiber: 1g; Sodium: 313mg

Moroccan Flank Steak with Harissa Couscous, *page 140*

# Meat

# Lamb and Bean Stew

Serves: **4** | Prep time: **15 minutes** | Cook time: **35 minutes**

This recipe comes directly from our Egyptian family friends. It's a delicious mixture of vegetables, beans, and lamb. The cut of lamb in this stew is very flavorful and often well marbled with fat, which means you might have to skim off a bit of fat from the top before serving. The best way to do this is to let the stew sit for 10 minutes and then lay paper towels on the surface to soak up the fat layer that floats up. Discard the paper towels and enjoy.

4 tablespoons olive oil, divided

1 pound lamb shoulder, cut into 2-inch cubes

Sea salt

Freshly ground black pepper

2 garlic cloves, minced (optional)

1 large onion, diced

1 cup chopped celery

1 cup chopped tomatoes

1 cup chopped carrots

⅓ cup tomato paste

1 (28-ounce) can white kidney beans, drained and rinsed

2 cups water

1. In a stockpot, heat 1 tablespoon of olive oil over medium-high heat. Season the lamb pieces with salt and pepper and add to the stockpot with the garlic, if desired. Brown the lamb, turning it frequently, for 3 to 4 minutes. Add the remaining 3 tablespoons of olive oil, the onion, celery, tomatoes, and carrots and cook for 4 to 5 minutes.

2. Add the tomato paste and stir to combine, then add the beans and water. Bring the mixture to a boil, reduce the heat to low, cover, and simmer for 25 minutes, or until the lamb is fully cooked.

3. Taste, adjust the seasoning, and serve.

**STORAGE:** Store leftovers in an airtight container in the refrigerator for up to 3 days.

**SUBSTITUTION TIP:** This recipe will also work with the same amount of beef chuck in place of the lamb. The cooking time should be the same.

Per serving: Calories: 521; Total fat: 24g; Total carbs: 43g; Sugar: 8g; Protein: 36g; Fiber: 12g; Sodium: 140mg

# Roasted Leg of Lamb with Potatoes

Serves: **6** | Prep time: **10 minutes** | Cook time: **3 hours**

Although this recipe may have one of the longest cooking times in this book, it's well worth it. Roasted lamb is perfect for a weekend meal, and the leftovers can be eaten throughout the week. The garlic, lemon, and oregano blend so nicely with the lamb, and the potatoes soak up all the juices, creating flavor explosions in every bite.

1 (5-pound) leg of lamb
1 to 2 tablespoons olive
  oil, for drizzling
Juice of 3 lemons,
  divided
1 teaspoon dried
  oregano, plus extra

for sprinkling
  over potatoes
½ teaspoon dried
  rosemary, plus
  extra for sprinkling
  over potatoes
3 garlic cloves, minced
Sea salt

Freshly ground
  black pepper
3½ pounds red
  potatoes, cut into
  1-inch chunks
3 tablespoons
  unsalted butter
½ cup water

1. Preheat the oven to 300°F.

2. Rinse the leg of lamb with cold water and place it in a roasting pan, fat-side up. Drizzle the lamb with the olive oil and sprinkle with the juice of 1 lemon. Sprinkle with the oregano, rosemary, and garlic and season with salt and pepper.

3. Place the lamb in the oven and bake for about 2 hours, rotating and basting it periodically. If the pan gets too dry, add a little water.

4. Remove the pan from the oven and increase the oven temperature to 350°F. Spread the potatoes around the lamb and drizzle the juice of the remaining 2 lemons over them. Sprinkle the potatoes with a little oregano and rosemary and season with salt and pepper. Place dabs of the butter all over the potatoes and pour in the water.

CONTINUES >

5. Place the roasting pan back in the oven and bake for about 1 hour, until the lamb is cooked to your desired doneness (an internal temperature of about 145°F indicates medium doneness) and the potatoes are tender.

6. Remove from the oven, slice the lamb, and serve with the potatoes.

STORAGE: Store leftovers in an airtight container in the refrigerator for up to 3 days.

COOKING TIP: No need to use a roasting rack—let all ingredients cook together in the pan. Use a meat thermometer to determine when the lamb is done to your liking. The potatoes will absorb all the flavors from the lamb, so no need to overcompensate with extra herbs.

Per serving: Calories: 771; Total fat: 28g; Total carbs: 44g; Sugar: 4g; Protein: 81g; Fiber: 5g; Sodium: 365mg

# Lebanese Stuffed Cabbage Rolls

Serves: **5 or 6** | Prep time: **30 minutes** | Cook time: **60 minutes**

Cabbage rolls are a bit labor-intensive, but the finished dish is worth whatever time you spend putting it together. Some variation of this recipe can be found in different countries all throughout the Mediterranean region. The ingredients are inexpensive, and the meat mixture absorbs all the spices, herbs, and vegetable juices, so the rolls are bursting with flavor. You can create different versions every time you make the rolls by altering the grain, seasonings, and meat you use.

1 teaspoon sea salt

2 heads cabbage, cored

2 pounds lean ground
  beef or lamb

1¼ cups uncooked
  white rice

1 cup olive oil

½ onion, chopped

2 teaspoons
  ground cinnamon

Sea salt

Freshly ground
  black pepper

2 cups water

3 tablespoons
  tomato paste

1 chicken bouillon cube

1. In a large stockpot, combine 10 to 12 cups water with the salt and bring to a boil over high heat. Add the cabbage; as the heads boil and the leaves loosen, remove each leaf and set it aside in a bowl of ice water. Once all leaves have been separated, drain them and set aside.

2. In a large bowl, mix together the ground beef, rice, olive oil, onion, and cinnamon until well combined. Season with salt and pepper and mix again.

3. In a medium bowl, stir together the water, tomato paste, and bouillon cube and set aside.

4. Place a spoonful of the meat mixture in the center of a cabbage leaf, fold the sides over the filling, and roll it up from one of the open sides to create a tight roll. Place the cabbage roll seam-side down in the now-empty stockpot and repeat until you have used all the meat mixture.

CONTINUES >

5. Pour the tomato mixture into the pot; it should reach about 1 inch below the top layer of cabbage rolls.

6. Place the stockpot over medium-high heat and bring to a boil, then reduce the heat to low, cover, and simmer for 1 hour. Serve.

STORAGE: Store leftovers in an airtight container in the refrigerator for up to 3 days.

COOKING TIP: To core the cabbage while leaving it otherwise intact, use a sharp knife to cut a square 5 to 6 inches deep around the core and pull it out. Stick a fork in the hole where the core was and use it to move the cabbage head in and out of the water to avoid burning yourself.

Per serving: Calories: 888; Total fat: 53g; Total carbs: 60g; Sugar: 11g; Protein: 46g; Fiber: 10g; Sodium: 235mg

# Greek Meatball Soup | Youvarlakia Avgolemono

Serves: **5** | Prep time: **20 minutes** | Cook time: **45 minutes**

Avgolemono makes another appearance in this comforting soup. The meatballs pack a delicious herbal punch, and the lemony broth brings it together for a meal the whole family will enjoy. Oregano and other herbs will work here, so feel free to get creative.

1 pound ground beef

⅓ cup orzo

4 large eggs

1 onion, finely chopped

2 garlic cloves, minced

2 tablespoons finely chopped fresh Italian parsley

Sea salt

Freshly ground black pepper

½ cup all-purpose flour

5 to 6 cups chicken broth

Juice of 2 lemons

1. In a large bowl, combine the ground beef, orzo, 1 egg, the onion, garlic, and parsley and stir until well mixed. Season with salt and pepper and mix again.

2. Place the flour in a small bowl.

3. Roll the meat mixture into a ball about the size of a golf ball and dredge it in the flour to coat, shaking off any excess. Place the meatball in a stockpot and repeat with the remaining meat mixture.

4. Pour enough broth into the pot to cover the meatballs by about 1 inch. Bring the broth to a boil over high heat. Reduce the heat to low, cover, and simmer for 30 to 45 minutes, until the meatballs are cooked through.

5. While the meatballs are simmering, in a small bowl, whisk the 3 remaining eggs until frothy. Add the lemon juice and whisk well.

6. When the meatballs are cooked, while whisking continuously, slowly pour 1½ cups of the hot broth into the egg mixture. Pour the egg mixture back

CONTINUES >

into the pot and mix well. Bring back to a simmer, then remove from the heat and serve.

**STORAGE:** Store leftovers in an airtight container in the refrigerator for up to 3 days.

**VARIATION TIP:** This recipe works with ground turkey or lamb in place of the ground beef. If using turkey, try increasing the quantity of herbs slightly to impart more flavors.

Per serving: Calories: 297; Total fat: 9g; Total carbs: 28g; Sugar: 4g; Protein: 27g; Fiber: 1g; Sodium: 155mg

# Traditional Ragù

Serves: **4 or 5** | Prep time: **15 minutes** | Cook time: **1 hour 30 minutes**

An Italian friend gave us this recipe years ago, and we've been cooking it ever since. In this sauce, the focus is on the meat, which adds flavor and texture. This is not just a standard tomato-based pasta topper—try spooning it over vegetables, bread, potatoes, or anything else it could enhance.

3 tablespoons unsalted butter

2 tablespoons olive oil

2 bay leaves

1 pound ground beef

½ cup good red wine

½ onion, finely chopped

1 medium carrot, finely chopped

1 teaspoon chopped fresh rosemary

½ cup chopped fresh Italian parsley

1 (14-ounce) can tomato sauce

1½ teaspoons tomato paste

Sea salt

Freshly ground black pepper

Cooked pasta, for serving

1. In a stockpot, heat the butter, olive oil, and bay leaves over medium heat. Add the ground beef and cook, stirring occasionally, until browned, 5 to 7 minutes. Increase the heat to high and add the wine. Cook for 4 to 5 minutes, until it reduces by about three-quarters.

2. Add the onion, carrot, rosemary, parsley, tomato sauce, and tomato paste and stir to combine. Reduce the heat to low, cover, and simmer for about 1 hour, stirring every 10 to 15 minutes.

3. Season with salt and pepper and serve over your favorite pasta.

**STORAGE:** Store leftover sauce in an airtight container in the refrigerator for up to 4 days or in the freezer for up to 3 weeks.

**SERVING TIP:** The wine you use will impart a distinct flavor to the sauce, so choose a bottle you like to drink.

Per serving: Calories: 346; Total fat: 21g; Total carbs: 10g; Sugar: 5g; Protein: 26g; Fiber: 3g; Sodium: 210mg

# Beef, Mushroom, and Green Bean Soup

Serves: **4** | Prep time: **10 minutes** | Cook time: **45 minutes**

This hearty recipe really highlights the mixture of meat and vegetables in the Mediterranean diet. It's our go-to when we have fresh green beans in the refrigerator. Throw the soup together on a crisp fall day and serve it with a thick slab of bread.

2 tablespoons olive oil

1 pound chuck or round beef roast, cut into 2-inch pieces

1 large onion, diced

½ teaspoon sea salt

¼ teaspoon freshly ground black pepper

½ cup white wine

8 cups chicken broth

1 pound green beans

8 ounces cremini (baby bella) mushrooms, chopped

3 tablespoons tomato paste

½ teaspoon dried oregano

1. In a large stockpot, heat the olive oil over medium-high heat. Add the beef and brown, 5 to 7 minutes. Add the onion, salt, and pepper and cook for 5 minutes. Add the wine and cook for 4 minutes. Add the broth, green beans, mushrooms, tomato paste, and oregano and stir to combine.

2. Bring to a boil, reduce the heat to low, cover, and simmer for 35 to 45 minutes, until the meat is cooked through. Serve.

**STORAGE:** Store leftovers in an airtight container in the refrigerator for up to 4 days.

**SUBSTITUTION TIP:** Lamb is an excellent substitute for the beef in this recipe.

Per serving: Calories: 307; Total fat: 14g; Total carbs: 17g; Sugar: 8g; Protein: 28g; Fiber: 5g; Sodium: 265mg

# Pork Stew with Leeks

Serves: **4** | Prep time: **15 minutes** | Cook time: **55 minutes**

Leeks are an exceptional vegetable and in season from fall to early winter. Look for smaller leeks because they are more tender and have a slightly sweeter flavor. This pork dish takes on the broth's taste to deliver an explosion of flavors in every bite.

2 tablespoons olive oil

2 leeks, white parts only, chopped and rinsed well

1 onion, chopped

2 garlic cloves, minced

1 carrot, chopped

1 celery stalk, chopped

2 pounds boneless pork loin chops, cut into 2-inch pieces

4 cups beef broth

2 cups water

3 potatoes, peeled and chopped

1 tablespoon tomato paste

Sea salt

Freshly ground black pepper

1. In a large skillet, heat the olive oil over medium-high heat. Add the leeks, onion, and garlic and sauté for 5 minutes, or until softened. Add the carrot and celery and cook for 3 minutes. Add the pork, broth, water, potatoes, and tomato paste and bring to a boil.

2. Reduce the heat to low, cover, and simmer for 45 minutes, or until the pork is cooked through. Season to taste with salt and pepper and serve.

**STORAGE:** Store leftovers in an airtight container in the refrigerator for up to 3 days.

**SUBSTITUTION TIP:** This stew would be nice with lamb, beef, or chicken if you prefer those proteins to pork.

Per serving: Calories: 623; Total fat: 16g; Total carbs: 60g; Sugar: 6g; Protein: 57g; Fiber: 8g; Sodium: 193mg

# Round Steak with Lemon Pepper

Serves: **4** | Prep time: **5 minutes** | Cook time: **10 minutes** | **5-Ingredient** | **30-Minute**

Sometimes the simplest ingredients create the most impressive meals. Lemon pepper is a classic pairing that really brings a dish to life, in this case accentuating the natural flavors of vegetables and meat. A little goes a long way, so don't overdo it or you will overpower the dish.

2 teaspoons lemon pepper seasoning
½ teaspoon garlic powder

4 beef round steaks (about 1½ pounds total)
1 tablespoon olive oil

Vegetables of your choice, for serving

1. In a small bowl, stir together the lemon pepper seasoning and garlic powder. Season the steaks all over with the mixture.

2. In a large skillet, heat the olive oil over medium-high heat. Add the steaks and cook for 4 to 5 minutes on each side.

3. Serve with vegetables alongside.

**STORAGE:** Store leftover steak in an airtight container in the refrigerator for up to 3 days.

**SUBSTITUTION TIP:** Different cuts of steak can be used instead of round steaks. Try sirloin or rib-eye steaks and adjust the cooking time as needed.

Per serving: Calories: 310; Total fat: 16g; Total carbs: 0g; Sugar: 0g; Protein: 38g; Fiber: 0g; Sodium: 107mg

# Greek Meatballs | Keftedes

Serves: **4 or 5** | Prep time: **15 minutes** | Cook time: **10 minutes** | **30-Minute**

Who doesn't like meatballs? Almost every country in the world has some version of these charming little meat bundles. This version is phenomenal served with some dipping sauce (think tzatziki, like the one on page 35, or your favorite dip). These meatballs pack a flavor punch, and the mint and lamb work so well together.

4 slices white bread, cut into ¼-inch chunks

3 tablespoons milk

1 medium onion, chopped

3 garlic cloves, minced

2 tablespoons dried mint

1 teaspoon sea salt

¼ teaspoon freshly ground black pepper

1 pound ground lamb

2 large eggs

½ cup all-purpose flour

⅓ cup olive oil, for frying

1. In a large bowl, combine the bread and milk and set aside.

2. In a food processor, combine the onion, garlic, mint, salt, and pepper and pulse until the onion is finely chopped. Add the onion mixture to the bowl with the milk and bread, then add the ground lamb and eggs and mix everything together.

3. Place the flour in a small bowl.

4. Form the meat mixture into balls about 2 inches in diameter, dredge them in the flour to coat, and shake off any excess. Set the meatballs on a plate as you form and dredge them.

5. In a large skillet, heat the olive oil over medium-high heat. Add the meatballs and cook, turning occasionally, until cooked through and browned, 7 to 10 minutes. Transfer the meatballs to a paper towel–lined plate to drain, then serve.

**STORAGE:** Store leftover meatballs in an airtight container in the refrigerator for up to 3 days.

**SUBSTITUTION TIP:** Oregano is a good substitute for mint if you're not a fan. Also, if you don't have lamb, use an equal quantity of ground beef.

Per serving: Calories: 459; Total fat: 24g; Total carbs: 28g; Sugar: 3g; Protein: 32g; Fiber: 4g; Sodium: 531mg

# Lebanese Ground Meat with Rice

Serves: **6** | Prep time: **10 minutes** | Cook time: **35 minutes**

This recipe is inspired by *hashweh*, an uncomplicated Lebanese dish of rice, ground meat, and spices. Here we've added mushrooms to give it a little extra something.

3 tablespoons olive
  oil, divided
4 ounces cremini
  (baby bella)
  mushrooms, sliced
½ red onion,
  finely chopped
2 garlic cloves, minced
1 pound lean
  ground beef

¾ teaspoon
  ground cinnamon
¼ teaspoon
  ground cloves
¼ teaspoon
  ground nutmeg
Sea salt
Freshly ground
  black pepper

1½ cups basmati rice
2¾ cups chicken broth
½ cup pine nuts
½ cup coarsely chopped
  fresh Italian parsley

1. In a sauté pan, heat 2 tablespoons of olive oil over medium-high heat. Add the mushrooms, onion, and garlic and sauté until the mushrooms release their liquid and the onion becomes translucent, about 5 minutes. Add the ground beef, cinnamon, cloves, and nutmeg and season with salt and pepper. Reduce the heat to medium and cook, stirring often, for 5 to 7 minutes, until the meat is cooked through. Remove the beef mixture from the pan with a slotted spoon and set aside in a medium bowl.

2. In the same pan, heat the remaining 1 tablespoon of olive oil over medium-high heat. Add the rice and fry for about 5 minutes. Return the meat mixture to the pan and mix well to combine with the rice. Add the broth and bring to a boil, then reduce the heat to low, cover, and simmer for 15 minutes, or until you can fluff the rice with a fork.

3. Add the pine nuts and mix well. Garnish with the parsley and serve.

**STORAGE:** Store leftovers in an airtight container in the refrigerator for up to 3 days or in the freezer for up to 2 weeks.

**SERVING TIP:** You can use quinoa or bulgur instead of the rice, if you prefer.

Per serving: Calories: 422; Total fat: 19g; Total carbs: 43g; Sugar: 1g; Protein: 22g; Fiber: 2g; Sodium: 81mg

# Pork with Orzo

Serves: **4** | Prep time: **10 minutes** | Cook time: **30 minutes**

Orzo has a splendid creamy texture when cooked, and when it's combined with tender pork and vegetables, your guests will beg for second helpings. Arugula adds a splash of color and a pleasing, slightly bitter taste. Although Parmesan is optional, the addition of cheese makes this dish exceptional.

2 tablespoons olive oil

2 yellow squash, diced

2 carrots, chopped

½ red onion, chopped

2 garlic cloves, minced

1 pound boneless pork loin chops, cut into 2-inch pieces

1 teaspoon Italian seasoning

2 cups chicken broth

1 cup dried orzo

2 cups arugula

Sea salt

Freshly ground black pepper

Grated Parmesan cheese (optional)

1. In a Dutch oven, heat the olive oil over medium-high heat. Add the squash, carrots, onion, and garlic and sauté for 5 minutes, or until softened. Add the pork and Italian seasoning and sauté, stirring occasionally, for 3 to 5 minutes, until browned.

2. Increase the heat to high, add the broth, and bring to a boil. Add the orzo, reduce the heat to medium-low, and simmer, stirring occasionally, for 8 minutes. Add the arugula and stir until wilted. Turn off the heat, cover, and let sit for 5 minutes.

3. Season with salt and pepper and serve topped with Parmesan, if desired.

**STORAGE:** Store leftovers in an airtight container in the refrigerator for up to 3 days or the freezer for 2 weeks.

**SUBSTITUTION TIP:** Feel free to substitute spinach for the arugula.

Per serving: Calories: 423; Total fat: 11g; Total carbs: 48g; Sugar: 5g; Protein: 31g; Fiber: 4g; Sodium: 127mg

# Moroccan Flank Steak with Harissa Couscous

Serves: **4** | Prep time: **5 minutes** | Cook time: **15 minutes** | **30-Minute**

This dish is a blend of North African flavors using a ton of spices and some heat to keep you coming back for more. Flank steak is considered a tough cut of beef, but it is also one of the most flavorful. The trick to a perfect flank steak is to avoid overcooking the meat, and always cut it thinly across the grain to break up its long muscle fibers.

1½ teaspoons coriander seeds

1¼ teaspoons ground ginger

½ teaspoon ground cumin

¾ teaspoon ground cinnamon

¼ teaspoon ground cloves

1½ pounds flank steak

3 tablespoons olive oil

¾ cup chicken broth

1 tablespoon harissa

½ cup chopped pitted dried dates

1 cup uncooked couscous

Sea salt

Freshly ground black pepper

¼ cup chopped fresh Italian parsley

1. In a small bowl, combine the coriander, ginger, cumin, cinnamon, and cloves. Rub the steak all over with the seasoning mix.

2. In a large sauté pan, heat the olive oil over medium-high heat. Add the steak and cook for 2 to 3 minutes on each side for medium-rare. Transfer the steak to a plate and set aside to rest for 10 minutes.

3. In the same pan, mix together the meat juices with the broth, harissa, and dates. Bring to a boil over medium-high heat. Add the couscous, remove from the heat, cover, and let stand for 5 minutes. Season with salt and pepper.

4. Cut the steak across the grain into thin strips.

5. Serve the steak with the couscous, garnished with parsley.

**STORAGE:** Store leftovers in an airtight container in the refrigerator for up to 4 days.

**VARIATION TIP:** Flank steaks can be marinated before cooking to improve their texture and add a lovely flavor. If you have a favorite marinade, use that instead of the seasoning blend.

**INGREDIENT TIP:** Different brands of harissa can vary wildly in flavor and heat, so you may not need to incorporate a full tablespoon, especially if yours is very spicy; you can always add more at the end to taste.

Per serving: Calories: 516; Total fat: 16g; Total carbs: 49g; Sugar: 12g; Protein: 43g; Fiber: 4g; Sodium: 137mg

Pistachio Cookies, *page 149*

# Desserts

# Toasted Almonds with Honey

Serves: **4** | Prep time: **15 minutes** | Cook time: **5 minutes** | **5-Ingredient** | **30-Minute**

Honey and toasted almonds pair so beautifully, you'll wonder why you ever ate one without the other. Removing the skin on the almonds boosts their flavor and improves the texture. Always choose exceptional honey because its flavor will make or break this dish.

½ cup raw almonds

3 tablespoons good-quality honey, plus more if desired

1. Fill a medium saucepan three-quarters full with water and bring to a boil over high heat. Add the almonds and cook for 1 minute. Drain the almonds in a fine-mesh sieve and rinse them under cold water to cool and stop the cooking. Remove the skins from the almonds by rubbing them in a clean kitchen towel. Place the almonds on a paper towel to dry.

2. In the same saucepan, combine the almonds and honey and cook over medium heat until the almonds get a little golden, 4 to 5 minutes. Remove from the heat and let cool completely, about 15 minutes, before serving or storing.

**STORAGE:** Store in an airtight container at room temperature for up to 3 days.

**VARIATION TIP:** Slivered almonds or shelled pistachios (or your favorite nuts) can be substituted here as well.

Per serving: Calories: 151; Total fat: 9g; Total carbs: 17g; Sugar: 14g; Protein: 4g; Fiber: 2g; Sodium: 1mg

# Cretan Cheese Pancakes

Serves: **4** | Prep time: **15 minutes** | Cook time: **25 minutes**

We had this unique dish on the Greek island of Crete. This recipe is how we captured that wonderful experience. The texture is more like fried bread than pancake, but you will still be reminded of pancakes as you drizzle on sweet honey.

2 cups all-purpose flour, plus extra for kneading

½ cup water

2 tablespoons olive oil, plus extra for frying

1 tablespoon freshly squeezed lemon juice

1 tablespoon brandy

1 teaspoon sea salt

5 tablespoons crumbled feta cheese

2 tablespoons olive oil

½ cup chopped nuts of your choice

⅛ to ¼ teaspoon ground cinnamon, for topping

1 tablespoon honey, for drizzling

1. In a large bowl, stir together the flour, water, olive oil, lemon juice, brandy, and salt until a ball of dough forms. Turn the dough out onto a lightly floured surface and knead for 10 minutes. If the dough is too wet, add a little more flour. If it's too dry, add some water.

2. Divide the dough into 5 equal pieces and roll each piece into a ball. Place a dough ball on a lightly floured surface and roll it out into a 6-inch-wide circle about ¼ inch thick. Place 1 tablespoon of the feta in the center, fold the dough over, and knead the dough and cheese together. Once the cheese is well incorporated, roll the dough out flat to the same size. Repeat with the remaining balls of dough.

3. In a large skillet, heat the oil over medium-high heat. Place one round of dough in the skillet and cook for 5 to 6 minutes on each side, until golden brown. Transfer the cooked pancake to a paper towel–lined plate to drain. Repeat to cook the remaining dough pancakes.

4. Sprinkle the pancakes evenly with the nuts and cinnamon, drizzle with the honey, and serve.

STORAGE: Store leftovers in an airtight container in the refrigerator for up to 3 days.

Per serving: Calories: 480; Total fat: 24g; Total carbs: 57g; Sugar: 6g; Protein: 11g; Fiber: 3g; Sodium: 396mg

# Fruit with Mint and Crème Fraîche

Serves: **4** | Prep time: **10 minutes** | **No-Cook** | **5-Ingredient** | **30-Minute**

In many Mediterranean regions, fresh fruit is served with every meal and often as a dessert. The simple, fresh flavors of ripe melon and sweet berries are decadent enough to be an end-of-meal indulgence. This colorful dessert with its fresh minty accent is perfect after a heavy meal. Feel free to use your favorite fruit or whatever you have in the refrigerator.

4 cups chopped fresh fruit (such as strawberries, honeydew, cantaloupe, watermelon, and blueberries)

1 cup crème fraîche
1 teaspoon sugar (optional)

¼ cup chopped fresh mint leaves, plus mint sprigs for garnish

1.  Evenly divide the fruit among four bowls.

2.  In a small bowl, mix the crème fraîche and sugar, if desired. Top the fruit with a generous spoonful or two of the crème fraîche.

3.  Sprinkle the mint over each bowl, garnish with 1 to 2 whole sprigs of mint, and serve.

**VARIATION TIP:** Add lemon zest to the crème fraîche for a bit of kick. Feel free to add more or less sugar (or none at all) depending on your preference.

Per serving: Calories: 164; Total fat: 12g; Total carbs: 14g; Sugar: 10g; Protein: 2g; Fiber: 3g; Sodium: 29mg

# Greek Honey-Cinnamon Doughnuts

Serves: **5 or 6** | Prep time: **1 hour 20 minutes** | Cook time: **4 minutes**

Known as *loukoumades*, these delicious fried dough balls are heavenly. The puffy dough soaks up all the delightful honey syrup, and chopped nuts elevate this dessert to greatness. Toasted sesame seeds are also a traditional topping for these golden treats.

3½ cups all-purpose flour

1 cup warm water

1 (¼-ounce) packet instant yeast

1 cup milk

2 large eggs

¼ cup sugar

1 teaspoon sea salt

1 cup water

¾ cup honey

4 cups safflower oil, for frying (enough for the dough balls to float)

¼ teaspoon ground cinnamon, for topping

¼ cup chopped nuts of your choice, for topping (optional)

1. In a large bowl, stir together the flour, warm water, and yeast and mix well. Add the milk, eggs, sugar, and salt and mix until a thick batter is formed. Cover the batter and let it rest for 45 to 60 minutes.

2. When the batter has about 20 minutes of resting time left, in a large saucepan, stir together the water and honey and bring to a simmer over medium heat. Simmer for 5 minutes, then remove from the heat and pour into a medium bowl.

3. Rinse and dry the saucepan. Pour in the safflower oil and heat over medium-high heat.

4. When the oil is hot, scoop 1 tablespoon of batter, form it into a ball, and gently drop it into the hot oil. Fry for 3 to 4 minutes on each side until golden brown. Transfer the doughnut to a paper towel–lined plate to drain and repeat to fry the remaining batter.

5. Add the fried doughnuts to the honey mixture, coating them evenly, then transfer them to a plate. Dust with the cinnamon, top with chopped nuts, if desired, and serve immediately.

Per serving: Calories: 677; Total fat: 16g; Total carbs: 122g; Sugar: 54g; Protein: 14g; Fiber: 3g; Sodium: 287mg

# Greek Yogurt with Honey and Pomegranates

Serves: **4** | Prep time: **5 minutes** | **No-Cook** | **5-Ingredient** | **30-Minute**

When in season, pomegranates are our first choice of fruit. The trick to eating this tart-sweet fruit is to cut them in half and submerge them in water to remove their seeds. Their flavor works well with golden honey, and if you need a bit more sweetness, sprinkle a little sugar on top as the crowning touch.

4 cups plain full-fat Greek yogurt

½ cup pomegranate seeds

¼ cup honey

Sugar, for topping (optional)

1. Evenly divide the yogurt among four bowls. Evenly divide the pomegranate seeds among the bowls and drizzle each with the honey.

2. Sprinkle each bowl with a pinch of sugar, if desired, and serve.

Per serving: Calories: 232; Total fat: 8g; Total carbs: 33g; Sugar: 32g; Protein: 9g; Fiber: 1g; Sodium: 114mg

# Pistachio Cookies

Serves: **6** | Prep time: **20 minutes** | Cook time: **12 minutes**

Some may argue that these pistachio-flavored cookies have more of a biscuity consistency, but to us, they are delicious cookies. The addition of ground nuts creates a glorious tender texture and gives the cookies rich flavor. We make these a few times a year, and they're always a hit.

1 cup all-purpose flour, plus extra for dusting

¼ cup cornstarch

1 teaspoon baking powder

Pinch sea salt

1 large egg

½ cup confectioners' sugar

½ cup (1 stick) unsalted butter, at room temperature

½ teaspoon lemon zest

½ teaspoon pure vanilla extract

½ cup finely ground pistachios

1. Preheat the oven to 400°F. Line a baking sheet with parchment paper.

2. In a large bowl, stir the flour, cornstarch, baking powder, and salt until well blended.

3. Add the egg, confectioners' sugar, butter, lemon zest, and vanilla and stir until the dough is uniform.

4. Turn the dough out onto a lightly floured surface and flatten it out with your hands. Place the ground pistachios in the center of the dough and knead the dough to evenly incorporate the nuts.

5. Roll the dough into 2-inch balls and place them on the prepared baking sheet, then use your palm to flatten them slightly.

6. Bake the cookies for 10 to 12 minutes, until golden brown.

7. Remove the cookies from the oven and let cool before serving or storing.

**STORAGE:** Store in an airtight container at room temperature for up to 4 days.

**VARIATION TIP:** Walnuts can be used in addition to the pistachios for a unique treat, or used them to replace the pistachios altogether.

Per serving: Calories: 336; Total fat: 21g; Total carbs: 32g; Sugar: 9g; Protein: 5g; Fiber: 2g; Sodium: 161mg

# Grilled Peaches with Greek Yogurt

Serves: **4** | Prep time: **5 minutes** | Cook time: **30 minutes** | **5-Ingredient**

We love peaches, and when you grill or bake these gorgeous stone fruits, they release all their delicious natural sugars. This sweetness plays wonderfully well with the tartness of Greek yogurt. This simple dessert is one you can go back to time and time again when you feel like treating yourself. Since you're just eating fruit, have seconds!

4 ripe peaches, halved and pitted

2 tablespoons olive oil

1 teaspoon ground cinnamon, plus extra for topping

2 cups plain full-fat Greek yogurt

¼ cup honey, for drizzling

1. Preheat the oven to 350°F.

2. Place the peaches in a baking dish, cut-side up.

3. In a small bowl, stir together the olive oil and cinnamon, then brush the mixture over the peach halves.

4. Bake the peaches for about 30 minutes, until they are soft.

5. Top the peaches with the yogurt and drizzle them with the honey, then serve.

COOKING TIP: Instead of baking the peaches, you can grill them cut-side down over medium heat. Grilled peaches are delicious and make a perfect dessert to enjoy while lounging outside during the summer months.

Per serving: Calories: 259; Total fat: 11g; Total carbs: 38g; Sugar: 36g; Protein: 6g; Fiber: 3g; Sodium: 57mg

# Strawberry Ricotta Parfaits

Serves: **4** | Prep time: **10 minutes** | **No-Cook** | **5-Ingredient** | **30-Minute**

We had the dessert that inspired these parfaits years ago at a local Italian restaurant. It was so simple, yet delicious. We love making these parfaits in the summer when strawberries are in season and are at the peak of their flavor. Different types of honey derive their delightful flavors from the variety of flowers frequented by the bees who produce it. Try varieties such as alfalfa honey or lavender honey in this dish to change the character.

2 cups ricotta cheese
¼ cup honey

2 cups sliced
  strawberries
1 teaspoon sugar

Toppings such as
  sliced almonds, fresh
  mint, and lemon
  zest (optional)

1. In a medium bowl, whisk together the ricotta and honey until well blended. Place the bowl in the refrigerator for a few minutes to firm up the mixture.

2. In a medium bowl, toss together the strawberries and sugar.

3. In each of four small glasses, layer 1 tablespoon of the ricotta mixture, then top with a layer of the strawberries and finally another layer of the ricotta.

4. Finish with your preferred toppings, if desired, then serve.

Per serving: Calories: 311; Total fat: 16g; Total carbs: 29g; Sugar: 23g; Protein: 14g; Fiber: 2g; Sodium: 106mg

# Whipped Greek Yogurt with Chocolate

Serves: **4** | Prep time: **10 minutes** | **No-Cook** | **5-Ingredient** | **30-Minute**

This is a luscious healthy version of chocolate mousse. Whipping Greek yogurt is a unique way to create fabulous texture with an unexpected tangy taste. Chocolate is an obsession for many people, and even a delicate sprinkling of grated chocolate has an impact on the flavor of this dish. Chocolate, in moderation, is on the "healthy foods" list in the Mediterranean diet because of its high antioxidant content. Not all chocolate is created equal, though; to get all the health benefits, look for good-quality organic dark chocolate (at least 70% cacao), with no refined sugar or fillers.

4 cups plain full-fat Greek yogurt

½ cup heavy (whipping) cream

2 ounces dark chocolate (at least 70% cacao), grated, for topping

1.  In the bowl of a stand mixer fitted with the whisk attachment or in a large bowl using a handheld mixer, whip the yogurt and cream for about 5 minutes, or until peaks form.

2.  Evenly divide the whipped yogurt mixture among bowls and top with the grated chocolate. Serve.

**PREP TIP:** If you do not have a mixer, you can whip the yogurt and cream together by hand with a whisk.

Per serving: Calories: 337; Total fat: 25g; Total carbs: 19g; Sugar: 16g; Protein: 10g; Fiber: 2g; Sodium: 127mg

# Churro Bites with Dark Chocolate Sauce

Serves: **6** | Prep time: **10 minutes** | Cook time: **35 minutes**

During our travels, we stumbled into a Spanish taverna owned by an amazing man from Granada, and ate the most delectable churros dipped in choco-late. The combination completely blew us away. This recipe brought us right back to that day, and we hope you love these churros as much as we do.

1 cup water

1 teaspoon pure
  vanilla extract

2 tablespoons
  unsalted butter

½ teaspoon sea salt

½ cup sugar, plus more
  for dredging

1 teaspoon ground
  cinnamon, plus more
  for dredging

1 cup all-purpose flour

2 cups safflower oil,
  for frying

2 large eggs

1 cup dark
  chocolate chips

¼ cup heavy
  (whipping) cream

1. In a medium saucepan, combine the water, vanilla, butter, salt, sugar, and cinnamon. Bring to a boil over high heat.

2. Reduce the heat to low and add the flour, then stir quickly until a ball of dough forms. Remove from the heat and let stand for 5 minutes.

3. Add the eggs to the dough one at a time, stirring after each addition until combined. Transfer the dough to a piping bag fitted with the tip of your choice (or put one large zip-top bag inside another, transfer the dough to the inner bag, and cut off one corner to make a hole for piping the dough).

4. Clean and dry the saucepan you used for the dough, then pour in the safflower oil and heat over high heat to 350°F.

5. To make bite-size pieces, pipe 2-inch-long strips of dough, then use a knife or fork to slice off the dough at the tip of the piping bag. Fry until golden on all sides, being careful not to overcrowd the pan, then transfer to a paper towel–lined plate to drain. Repeat to fry the remaining dough.

**CONTINUES >**

6.  Combine some sugar and cinnamon in a shallow bowl and dredge the churros in the mixture.

7.  In a small microwave-safe bowl, combine the chocolate chips and cream and microwave in 30-second intervals, stirring after each, until melted and well combined.

8.  Serve the churros immediately, with the chocolate sauce alongside.

VARIATION TIP: Add a pinch of espresso powder to the chocolate sauce to intensify its flavor.

Per serving: Calories: 429; Total fat: 26g; Total carbs: 42g; Sugar: 22g; Protein: 6g; Fiber: 3g; Sodium: 159mg

# Measurement Conversions

## VOLUME EQUIVALENTS (LIQUID)

| US Standard (ounces) | US Standard (approximate) | Metric |
|---|---|---|
| 2 tablespoons | 1 fl. oz. | 30 ml |
| ¼ cup | 2 fl. oz. | 60 ml |
| ½ cup | 4 fl. oz. | 120 ml |
| 1 cup | 8 fl. oz. | 240 ml |
| 1½ cups | 12 fl. oz. | 355 ml |
| 2 cups or 1 pint | 16 fl. oz. | 475 ml |
| 4 cups or 1 quart | 32 fl. oz. | 1 L |
| 1 gallon | 128 fl. oz. | 4 L |

## OVEN TEMPERATURES

| Fahrenheit (F) | Celsius (C) (approximate) |
|---|---|
| 250°F | 120°C |
| 300°F | 150°C |
| 325°F | 165°C |
| 350°F | 180°C |
| 375°F | 190°C |
| 400°F | 200°C |
| 425°F | 220°C |
| 450°F | 230°C |

## VOLUME EQUIVALENTS

| US Standard | Metric (approximate) |
|---|---|
| ⅛ teaspoon | 0.5 ml |
| ¼ teaspoon | 1 ml |
| ½ teaspoon | 2 ml |
| ¾ teaspoon | 4 ml |
| 1 teaspoon | 5 ml |
| 1 tablespoon | 15 ml |
| ¼ cup | 59 ml |
| ⅓ cup | 79 ml |
| ½ cup | 118 ml |
| ⅔ cup | 156 ml |
| ¾ cup | 177 ml |
| 1 cup | 235 ml |
| 2 cups or 1 pint | 475 ml |
| 3 cups | 700 ml |
| 4 cups or 1 quart | 1 L |

## WEIGHT EQUIVALENTS (DRY)

| US Standard | Metric (approximate) |
|---|---|
| ½ ounce | 15 g |
| 1 ounce | 30 g |
| 2 ounces | 60 g |
| 4 ounces | 115 g |
| 8 ounces | 225 g |
| 12 ounces | 340 g |
| 16 ounces or 1 pound | 455 g |

# References

Aizawa, Koichi, Toshihiro Matsumoto, Takahiro Inakuma, Tomoko Ishijima, Yuji Nakai, Keiko Abe, and Fumio Amano. "Administration of Tomato and Paprika Beverages Modifies Hepatic Glucose and Lipid Metabolism in Mice: A DNA Microarray Analysis." *Journal of Agricultural and Food Chemistry* 57, no. 22 (November 25, 2009):10964–71. doi: 10.1021/jf902401u.

Hyman, Leslie, ed. "The Relationship of Dietary Carotenoid and Vitamin A, E, and C Intake with Age-Related Macular Degeneration in a Case-Control Study: AREDS Report no. 22." *Arch Opthalmology* 125, no. 9 (September 2007): 1225–32. doi: 10.1001/archopht.125.9.1225.

Mayo Clinic. "Mediterranean Diet: A Heart-Healthy Eating Plan." MayoClinic.org /healthy-lifestyle/nutrition-and-healthy-eating/in-depth/mediterranean-diet /art-20047801.

Sanati, Setareh, Bibi Marjan Razavi, and Hossein Hosseinzadeh. "A Review of the Effects of *Capsicum annuum* L. and Its Constituent, Capsaicin, in Metabolic Syndrome." *Iranian Journal of Basic Medical Sciences* 21, no. 5 (May 2018):439–448. doi: 10.22038/IJBMS.2018.25200.6238.

Trichopoulou, Antonia, Miguel A Martínez-González, Tammy YN Tong, Nita G Forouhi, Shweta Khandelwal, Dorairaj Prabhakaran, Dariush Mozaffarian, and Michel de Lorgeril. "Definitions and Potential Health Benefits of the Mediterranean Diet: Views from Experts around the World." *BMC Medicine* 12, no. 112 (2014). Published online July 24, 2014. doi: 10.1186/1741-7015-12-112.

# Index

# Acknowledgments

First and foremost, we want to thank our editor, Jed Bickman, and his team at Callisto Media for the tremendous time and effort they put into this project with us. Without them, this book wouldn't have been possible.

We want to thank all our family and friends who've supported us over the years. We also want to thank the many people we've met along our travels. From locals enthusiastic about their culture and foods to chefs from hole-in-the-wall places and well-known restaurants who've spoken to us, guided us, inspired us, and continue to elevate Mediterranean cuisine—thank you.

Lastly, we'd like to thank you, the reader, for deciding to explore Mediterranean foods and to see for yourself how simple ingredients can be not only healthy and cooked in one pot but also delicious. We hope you get as much joy from your healthy Mediterranean journey as we do.

# About the Authors

**Kenton** and **Jane Kotsiris** are food bloggers who specialize in exploring Greek and Mediterranean cuisine. They advocate eating healthy unprocessed foods and living a healthy lifestyle that can be maintained every day.

They are the authors of the popular Greek food blog *Lemon and Olives* and have written widely on the subject of Greek cuisine. Some of their works include *Top 10 Greek Dishes under 500 Calories* and *Cooking Like a Greek*. They received their bachelor's degrees from the University of California, Los Angeles (UCLA) and their master's degrees from the University of Sheffield in the United Kingdom.

They try to travel in the Mediterranean several months out of the year. Currently, they live in Orange County, California.